GOOD
CATASTROPHE

GOOD
CATASTROPHE

The Tide-Turning Power of Hope

BENJAMIN WINDLE

BETHANYHOUSE

a division of Baker Publishing Group
Minneapolis, Minnesota

© 2023 by Benjamin Windle

Published by Bethany House Publishers
Minneapolis, Minnesota
www.bethanyhouse.com

Bethany House Publishers is a division of
Baker Publishing Group, Grand Rapids, Michigan

Printed in the United States of America

Library of Congress Cataloging-in-Publication Data
ISBN 978-0-7642-4116-1 (paperback)
ISBN 978-0-7642-4163-5 (casebound)
ISBN 978-1-4934-4082-5 (ebook)
Library of Congress Control Number: 2022045381

Cover design by Dan Pitts

Author represented by The Fedd Agency, Inc.

Baker Publishing Group publications use paper produced from sustainable forestry practices and post-consumer waste whenever possible.

23   24   25   26   27   28   29   7   6   5   4   3   2   1

Contents

For there is hope for a tree,

    if it be cut down, that it will sprout again,

    and that its shoots will not cease.

Though its root grow old in the earth,

    and its stump die in the soil,

yet at the scent of water it will bud

    and put out branches like a young plant.

—Job 14:7–9 ESV

Introduction

What if we could fundamentally reframe how we see life's challenges?

The story that the "good life"—the life of happiness, success, and health—is somehow predicated on us eliminating problems, adversity, and challenges is not working.

We all experience pain in life. Uncertainty about the future is growing. The world feels fragile. Our stress, anxiety, and depression are at such acute levels that it seems we have to better understand the dark side of life in order to grab hold of the light.

Problems come in many shapes and sizes: they trespass into our homes, they blindside us in our relationships, they hijack our health, and they rob us of our finances. They are a ubiquitous part of our human experience, and this is why learning how hope can make a practical difference in our everyday lives is vitally important.

We have to get *good* at handling the *bad*.

What if pain and problems were not our enemies? What if the challenges we face in life were also the same things that shape us, define us, and take us to a new and brighter future? Can good come from our catastrophes?

It was through asking these questions that I was inspired by the story of a man named Job. He experienced devastating tragedies in his life. Yet, he exercised a form of hope so counterintuitive to his pain that even his closest friends were in awe of it. It was this hope that became the catalyst for a remarkable turnaround.

What if we could fundamentally reframe how we see life's challenges?

The closer I looked, the more I saw the story of Job as an unsolved puzzle.

In some ways, Job's story is dark, but it is also highly inspiring. I was captivated by this juxtaposition. In fact, what grabbed me—more than anything—was Job's use of a simple metaphor: of hope being like a tree that is cut down but then springs back to life at the scent of water. That phrase, *the scent of water*, crystallized in my mind as a symbol of a much bigger idea: our greatest challenges in life are inevitably linked to our greatest growth.

Even if your entire life is cut down to a stump that looks dead, new branches can grow, new flowers can bud, and new life can spring forth.

Using the ancient story of Job as a backdrop, this book provides a new perspective on many of the challenges you will face in modern life.

You will discover the secret to weathering life's storms, learn how to rise above daily imperfections, recognize where to turn in the midst of pain, find out how to survive crises and come out better, understand how to filter out worry and stress, and gain an ultimate perspective on every challenge you face in life.

You can end the quest for a trouble-free life and harness every adversity to your advantage.

True hope is more than a feeling or an emotion. It is real. It is a difference maker. And, if you continue reading, it can be yours today.

The deepest things that I have learned in my
own life have come from the deepest suffering.

—Elisabeth Elliot[1]

Stumptown

Expect new life to grow

"THERE'S BEEN A DOG ATTACK. Call an ambulance."

Even now, writing those words sucks the air out of my lungs. I can still feel the trauma surging through my nervous system.

My wife, Cindi, could barely speak as she walked into the front room of our house, clutching our youngest son in her arms. Her face was pale and had a look of complete terror on it.

A neighbor's unrestrained Rottweiler had violently mauled our seven-year-old son.

The little guy hadn't stood a chance against the beast. It had taken him by his neck and face. It had left him like a rag doll on the ground.

The damage took my breath away. The large laceration to the neck was clearly life-threatening. My son looked at me with panicked eyes and said, "Daddy, is this it?"

God, help me.

Help my son. If someone needs to go, please take me. I'll do anything—but just save my son.

This can't be how it ends.

My mind flashes back to the faces of the first responders. Their grave expressions. It's not good when you see fear in the eyes of the medical professionals. A wound of that magnitude along the neck could mean anything. And what would I know? I'm not a doctor. I just knew it was bad. Really bad. My body was in shock, and everything slowed down as stress chemicals surged through me.

As my youngest son was rushed to the hospital in the back of an ambulance, I knelt with my other two sons, held hands, and prayed that God would preserve his life. Pretty much everything else is a blur. As soon as other family members arrived, I rushed to the hospital to join my wife and son.

After a night in the emergency ward, we finally got a report from the doctors. They look for three kinds of damage with a wound like this. Tendons. Nerves. Arteries. The discovery? This attack miraculously missed all three. Yes, there's a scar and trauma, but the teeth were a millimeter off something infinitely more devastating.

Even today, I shudder thinking about this incident. The fragility of life assaults my mind.

I'm a father. I am meant to protect. But I couldn't protect against something I didn't see coming. What am I supposed to do? Live my life in constant anxiety, trying to anticipate any impending threat to my family? I've tried that, and a quick tip: that doesn't help anyone.

I've had so many questions since that day. Why didn't God cause the dog to be restrained? Why weren't we out of town? I think of about one hundred what-if variables that would lead to my son not being savaged. How can I live knowing that, at any time, something completely random can walk into my life and stab my soul with a dagger from behind? I guess that's the same circular vortex of thinking we all do when trying to make sense of the unthinkable.

My heart aches to think about this dog attack and my son. I mean, it really aches. I hate to think of the what-ifs. I hate that my wife had to witness it and try to pull the dog off. I hate remembering the look in my son's eyes when he looked up in fear for his life.

I hate the pain.

Physically, my little boy has made a truly inspiring recovery in the years since this attack. In fact, within the trauma, something sweet has developed.

I smile at his bravery when he went back to school and answered all the questions from his friends.

I smile at his resilience.

I smile at his continued love of dogs.

I've learned an important lesson about life and faith: God doesn't remove pain from our lives. He doesn't guard against its intrusion. I guess He could, but He doesn't. And for the life of me, I don't know why. Yes, I can give you all the explanations I was raised with about God—free will, eternal perspective, omniscient vs. finite reasoning. I mean, there are lots of explanations, and they are salves to the wounds life brings us. But the wounds still exist. Emotional devastation can hit us at any moment.

If I see the existence of pain as a conflict to hope, then I'm building my life on shallow sand. It may sound less confident, less full of faith, and less inspiring to actually admit to my human frailty. But this is where I've discovered something that is both counterintuitive and remarkable about hope. And it's this that I want to place in front of you.

If our idea of hope only works when our lives are as clear as summer, it can turn out to be a brittle worldview when the actual storms of life hit. I want to show you how hope and hardship collaborate in your flourishing.

A lot can turn in a week. Or a day. Or a single phone call.

How can life and the people we love be so fragile?

How can I stop myself from being overcome with feelings of dread or anxiety when I live with an awareness that everything that is most precious to me is outside of my ability to control or protect?

How can I handle the complexity of life, mental health, and the challenge of raising my three sons with my wife?

I think somewhere in an answer to this question needs to be a rediscovery of *hope*. In fact, I'm convinced of it. But in order to truly unleash hope in life's hardest fights, we need to redefine what it means.

> **We need a song that can be sung in the breathless shadows that tells us life is beautiful.**

I want you to know very early on in this conversation what my vantage point is. If you have breath in your lungs, then you have the capacity to have hope for a brighter tomorrow. At the same time, we are going to dismantle this idea that for hope to be real or powerful, we need to know the outcome or we need every blemish removed and every problem to disappear from our lives and never return. We know instinctively that this is not the human experience. Pain and problems will sit along with joy and laughter. So, we need an understanding of hope that can function in the reality of our broken human experience.

We need hope—but we need a hope that is robust enough to speak to real life. And cancer. And grief. And trauma. And doubt. And heartache. We need a song that can be sung in the breathless shadows that tells us life is beautiful.

Your troubles can fuel your turnaround.

Your destiny is linked to your despair.

Your pain can be used for your purpose.

Hope can be your difference maker.

One of the most fascinating examples of this is a person I've been reading and thinking about for many years: Job. The story of this man's life is remarkable, not because of its perfection but rather because of the interwoven themes of pain and hope. Let's get started.

The scent of water

Water. Can you smell it? The salty spray of an ocean shoreline. The earthy aroma of a running brook. The humid air before a thunderstorm.

To me, the scent of water is humble; it is neither overpowering nor obvious. In fact, it's almost hidden in the neon array of sensory experience that surrounds us. I guess that's what makes it such an interesting metaphor for describing hope.

The scent of coffee. The scent of buttered popcorn. The scent of freshly cut grass. These scents are all strong and recognizable.

So, why describe one of life's most essential themes with such a subtle choice? Why would a scent so faint, so hidden, be chosen by any writer to articulate the nature of hope? Yet, that's exactly the description chosen by a man who has come to embody the promise of hope amid great adversity. Job chose this metaphor from the well of bitterness.

Throughout the course of history, Job's life has almost become a fable, a flimsy caricature of a man who lived six thousand years ago. To truly learn modern lessons from Job's immense suffering, I decided that I needed to look closely at the real-life person at the center of this story. Feel his humanity. Connect with his pain. And it is here that I introduce you to this remarkable figure who embodied what we so desperately need today: a hope that thrives when life hurts.

Before tragedy struck, Job sat at the pinnacle of society. He was living the good life. Money. Power. Prestige. His business was booming—his herd numbered over ten thousand. He was happily married, and whenever he embraced his wife, his love for her overwhelmed him. Although they had lived much of their lives together, he still saw in her eyes the girl he first fell in love with. When he looked at his ten children, his heart filled with warmth. He remembered swaddling his babies on a cold night—looking into their eyes and dreaming of what they might become—and now he saw them strong and full of life.

Every few days, the family would all gather and eat dinner. Job would lean back in his chair, enjoying the laughter and banter of his children. It was everything he had ever dreamed of, and more. Even though he had become rich beyond measure, he had kept a humble heart and an authentic faith.

Then, one day, a perfect storm hit Job's life. Job was at home when a man came in and told him that his oxen and donkeys had been stolen by raiders and his staff murdered. At the same time, another messenger arrived, announcing that a fire killed all of Job's sheep, along with his shepherds. A third messenger told Job that thieves had stolen his camels. Tragically, a fourth messenger informed Job that all of his children were killed in a freak storm.

Job's health rapidly declined. Boils broke out all over his body. When Job's friends visited to comfort him, they barely recognized him—his pain had even altered his physical appearance. Job was a broken man.

His house was quiet.

No laughter.

No dinners with his sons and daughters.

Just pain.

Job's loss was so deep that even his tears were exhausted.

It's from *this* dark place that Job described his life as a tree. The tree was once flourishing; the roots spread wide and deep. The trunk extended li ke a tower into the sky. The leaves were green, and the flowers' perfumed scent filled the air. The tree—his life—was vibrant and strong.

Then the tree was brutally cut down.

Growth, fruit, life—all was stolen. The tree was dead, stripped bare, a shadow of what once existed.

A stump.

Although all appeared to be lost, Job made a prediction: at the scent of water, the stump would bud again like a flourishing tree.

Take note of Job's hopeful perspective amid his pain:

> For there is hope for a tree,
>> if it be cut down, that it will sprout again,
>> and that its shoots will not cease.
> Though its root grow old in the earth,
>> and its stump die in the soil,
> yet at the scent of water it will bud
>> and put out branches like a young plant.
>
> Job 14:7–9 ESV

Why is Job's picture of hope so delicate, so hidden, so soft? Perhaps that is the nature of hope; it must be searched for, its presence detected and encouraged. Yet, its power is so potent that even the smallest of doses can bring new life. The dead stump needed only the *scent* of water to bud again!

Scent-of-water moments are when our soul flickers with the hope that the insurmountable problems we are facing can shift in our favor. So often, my imagination is filled with feelings of fear or what-ifs about the future. But what would happen if we intentionally oriented our lives to try to detect the scent of water? If our hearts searched for even the softest hint of the tide-turning power of hope? Imagine what would happen if, right now, you started scanning for even the faintest scent of water in your life.

To search my own life for the scent of water, I asked myself this question: "What is my earliest memory of pain?" I had plenty of injuries and accidents growing up, burning myself on campfires and scratching my knee when I fell off my bicycle. Yet, my first memory is when I was very young. Maybe three years old. Spartanburg, South Carolina. I decided to open the door of a car that was traveling at nearly sixty miles per hour. To this day, I remember the feeling of tumbling out onto the hard, black asphalt.

Filled with terror, I was lying in the direct path of a large semitrailer truck that was coming the opposite way. Miraculously, the driver saw me, slammed on his brakes, stopped, and helped me to safety. I was bruised and shaken up, but otherwise fine. I had experienced pain. I remember it. Little did I know that it was a precursor to much of life itself. It was only later in life that I realized pain comes in ways we can't feel with our skin alone. Our souls can hurt, and our hearts can be bruised. But I also remember how there was hope even in that moment, and God turned the tide of pain to one of redemption.

Portland

I spent almost half of my twenties living in Portland, Oregon. It's a city of great coffee, a true foodie scene, and custodian of the motto "Keep Portland weird." Portland also has a nickname: *Stumptown*.

Ask a local today and you will see that the word *Stumptown* has become synonymous with a popular local coffee roaster that bears the same name (if you are ever in the area, you have to try it). Yet, the name has an older history. The origin of the name Stumptown dates back to the 1850s. The city was growing so rapidly that trees were cut down to make way for roads. Consequently, the forestry industry was booming, with vast tracts of the famed Oregon pine reduced to stumps—thus giving rise to Portland's nickname.

This analogy is a fitting tie-in to the concept we are talking about. What was once a forest teeming with wildlife is now a desolate land. The stumps offer a reminder of what once was. When I think of that image, it speaks to me about the story of our lives.

Our souls can become Stumptowns.

The stump is the life in need of hope.

It is the single mother struggling with the demands of raising kids.

It is the employee receiving a termination letter.

It is the star teen athlete who, in the last quarter of play, blows out their knee and their future.

It is the friendship that's on the brink of ending.

It is the marriage without romance.

It is the businessperson trying to cope with daily stress.

It is the shock of a terminal health diagnosis.

> **The capacity to dream again, to love again, and to soar again is at the heart of what it means to truly live.**

It is the harsh, unchanging reality of the death of a loved one.

It is the daily, gnawing feeling of insignificance, like a cloud that never recedes.

Can a life that has been cut down to the roots still survive?

Areas of my life have resembled barren stumps—from relationships to dreams to finances—and my experience is that the new, green shoots of life *can* and *do* sprout.

Job's life was a barren stump that grew back to life at the scent of water. The same can happen in *your* life. The capacity to dream again, to love again, and to soar again is at the heart of what it means to truly live.

Proverbs 13:12 says this: "Hope deferred makes the heart sick, but a dream fulfilled is a tree of life." Again we see the picture of a flourishing tree that is connected to hope. Live with expectation, and you will see life in a different light. I want you to take a moment to see your life as a flourishing tree and imagine buds sprouting and growing again.

Water

All of this made me think: What if the idea of a stump regenerating means more than the words themselves state? Is there any science behind Job's metaphor of the tree detecting the scent of water and flourishing back to life?

Can trees actually detect water?

My question led me to research conducted by scientists at the University of Western Australia. They found that plants possess complex and developed senses: they can discover—and even hear—water.

Lead researcher Dr. Monica Gagliano found that plants can sense sound vibrations from running water in the soil and grow their roots toward the source of water. In that sense, plants can *hear* water.[2] In fact, the hidden behavior of how trees draw water from the ground and transport it in special tissue (xylem) is still surrounded by much mystery and is the subject of cutting-edge studies. Trees are much more sophisticated than we generally assume.

The response that trees have to water is called *hydrotropism*. Perhaps Job's words were more than an analogy. Perhaps he was correlating a *biological* response he observed in plants to a *spiritual* response he saw in his life. If a tree can grow and stretch itself toward the possibility of water, perhaps the human soul can do the same—pushing its root system deeper and further in search of life.

Job said that a tree can flourish again at the "scent" of water. Notice how he did not say with the drenching of water, or with the flooding of nutrients. He wraps words around the idea that things can change with even the faintest aroma of the force we call hope.

Water brings life. To the thirsty traveler, a cool stream of fresh water offers sustenance. To the farmer who has planted seeds in dry soil, the opening of the heavens with a downpour of rain brings a future.

In ways you may not be fully conscious of, your soul is in search of this essential life source called hope. Even the slightest hint—the scent of water in the soil—causes a reaction within you of new life and growth. It doesn't take overwhelming evidence of better things ahead to trigger this growth: your soul can awaken with only a microscopic presence of hope.

Thankfully, Job's story didn't end at the stump. He regained his health, had more children, and grew his business beyond what it had been earlier. None of his later success erased the reality of what he had lost, but he lived again. He loved again. He believed again.

I'm moved whenever I read the narrative of Job's life. For me, it speaks to the human condition—the dilemmas and trials we all face—and an optimism that sees something positive in the future.

We all must answer this question: What do we do with our pain? Often, we handle our pain in the wrong ways—addiction, suppression, avoidance, withdrawal, and isolation. This, in turn, creates a well-worn path to a host of ailments, such as lack of sleep, burnout, stress, rumination, depression, anxiety, aching loneliness, spiritual bankruptcy, consumerism, and feelings of helplessness.

Something's broken, not just in how we process pain but in the fundamental way we see it and approach it.

And if we don't stop running from our problems, and if we don't start inviting hope into our shadows, we will miss out on one of the great transformative forces in our life. Yes, hope is more than a feeling. It is a practice, and in its most resilient form, hope is a worldview. It becomes the vantage point from which we see the entirety of our human experience.

It's human nature to avoid pain and try to eliminate problems, but there is a growing skepticism about the modern promise of a trouble-free life. Perhaps hardship and hope together can do something for us that a problem-free life never could. It's this idea that propelled me to look more deeply into the relationship between our destiny and our difficulties.

How we view pain and hope matters, because we spend a good portion of our lives carrying the weight of our trials. Hope that pretends these trials do not exist is functionally useless. True hope is not a comfortable idea. It does not shy away from the grey winters of life, but holds a promise of birdsong in spring. However, in our rush to make the idea more palatable, we have removed some of the grit of this virtue.

Perhaps hardship and hope together can do something for us that a problem-free life never could.

This conversation is not centered on surveying the full spectrum of Job's life. Hundreds of books do that. This book is focused on your life—your journey, your struggle, and the amazing possibility of your future. Are you facing challenges right now and asking, "Can God catch my falling tears? Will light ever burn its way into this darkness?" My message to you is this—every tree that is cut down in your life will flourish and bloom again with the scent of hope.

It's interesting that I find myself drawn to Job's pain. Maybe it's my growing distaste for overly simplistic platitudes about the "good life" that has made me hunt out ideas that can work, even when life is not postcard perfect. I don't want to just spray on a new coat of paint—I want to deal with the architecture of my soul.

When life doesn't go as planned, we often don't know how to respond. Without an understanding of how hope and pain coexist to bring about something special, we simply shove pain in a suitcase and carry it around with us, thinking it's locked away. But if we are honest, it's a constant burden. It takes up emotional real estate.

To talk about pain is not just a mechanical conversation. I don't approach it as an academic or philosophical subject. For me, talking about pain is personal. It's you and me and other real people going through real situations. It's not abstract; it has flesh and blood. Adversity is part of the human experience.

I don't have all the answers about why we face adversity and storms. I'm not sure why some people experience more trials than others. But what I do know, with absolute conviction, is that our world needs hope. In an era filled with confusion, anger, uncertainty, stress, volatility, and division, we need to learn how to build the virtue of hope into our homes, businesses, and hearts. No matter how deep the pain is, our ability to summon the courage to say "maybe, just maybe, there is something good for me in my future" is oxygen to the soul. Without hope, even if we had all the money and success in the world, would we really be *alive*?

Regardless of what storms you are facing right now, your life can bud and flourish again. Your life can change, even with the smallest measure of hope.

No matter how bleak, how discouraging, or how final your circumstances seem, stretch your expectations to believe that out of this situation, new opportunities will grow. Hope is a choice. An outlook. A posture of the soul. An attitude.

The picture of a barren stump flourishing back to health is the metaphoric masterpiece Job paints from his life. It says to me that things can turn around, no matter how hard life gets. In a valley? Mountaintops are on the horizon. In a storm? Rays of sun are about to break through the clouds. It's the song of life that doesn't end in silence but rather builds to a crescendo.

Stumptown? Or a field of potential? Know this: trees can grow again at the scent of water, and stumps can come back to life.

Life can bring much pain.

There are many ways to deal with this pain.

Choose wisely.

—J. Cole[1]

Saint Anne

Don't sanitize the mess

LEONARDO DA VINCI'S *The Virgin and Child with Saint Anne* is a masterpiece. This painting has been preserved for hundreds of years. It has survived wars, global upheaval, and natural disasters; it is truly priceless.

In order to present a brighter, more colorful image to the general-public, the Louvre, the magnificent museum in Paris, decided to clean the painting. But something went wrong. According to many, Leonardo's masterpiece was *overcleaned*. Its minor flaws were unnecessarily touched up. Cloudy dark shades now appeared bright and sunny.

When I read the story of this painting, it made me think of how it speaks to us about more than art. We live in a culture where we feel the pressure to present the best version of ourselves to the world. The gaps and the flaws are touched up. The shadows are brightened to sunshine. We, too, can be guilty of overcleaning what we put on display.

How often do we present a cleaned, brightened image of ourselves to others? We make the dark areas lighter. We remove the shadows. And, in doing so, we remove the depth.

This is particularly relevant to a conversation about hope, since there is a tendency to mistake hope for the notion that we must ignore our pain or the reality of our circumstances. But true hope is not hype. It's not pretending that everything is fine. Hardship, not perfection, is the starting point of hope. The trials of life are the catalysts for our growth and potential. The true power of hope can only begin to work at the point of authenticity.

When my son Houston was only a few months old, the doctors discovered he had a heart condition that required him to see a specialist. It felt like a storm had come out of nowhere. We were living in Oregon at the time, and I remember going to the large OHSU Children's Hospital that overlooks the downtown Portland area. Stainless steel. Fluorescent lighting. Long stark hallways. There's something about the clinical feel of a hospital corridor that stands in direct opposition to the situation at hand, which is raw, complex, and emotive.

But true hope is not hype. It's not pretending that everything is fine. Hardship, not perfection, is the starting point of hope.

While the doctors weren't too concerned about Houston, any parent knows that children's hospital visits are nerve-racking, to say the least. What-if questions swirled in my mind: *What if things are not okay? What if something goes wrong?*

However, as I sat in the waiting room that day, my questions seemed to fade as I looked at the other parents around me. Unlike Houston, the children of these parents were visibly sick. Some had shaved heads, a telltale sign of cancer treatment. Others were terribly skinny, their little bodies ravaged by disease. My heart broke, convinced that no suffering in the world is worse than that of a child's. Houston's heart turned out to be fine, but to this day I remember the sense of anguish I felt at not being able to control the outcome. What my soul needed was hope.

It makes me think of our story of Job through the lens of fatherhood.

What did Job think when he got the first knock on the door from the messenger with the tragic news about his family? It's like when someone calls and says, "I've got some bad news; you'd better sit down for this." For me, as a father and as a husband, I know my gut-level reaction at that moment: Are my wife and kids okay? Are they alive? Are they safe? From an instinctive part of my being, I know if my family is safe, I can deal with pretty much anything else. I can cope with a big tax bill, a deal falling through, or even personal sickness.

But my kids. Let my kids be okay.

So, how could Job possibly process the trauma of what he heard that day?

Business lost.

House destroyed.

But Job . . . it's your kids. They are all dead. They are gone. Something shocking and unspeakable has happened. They are not coming home.

We don't really get a window into Job's most immediate response, but we know his world folded in on top of him. You can rebuild a business, find a new job, pivot and adjust your life. But your kids? I know firsthand that it is the most vulnerable place in a father's heart. It's the gap in the armor that can be pierced by an arrow.

Did Job go emotionally numb?

Was something damaged in the very core of his being?

Did his brain chemistry change from the horrific shock?

Did he become frozen in hopelessness?

Was his grief process linear, or was it a swirl of unpredictable waves crashing over his heart?

Where do you turn when you're in distress? What if there is no one who can solve your problem? When you come to the end of yourself—your influence, your connections, your intelligence—then what? What do we do with pain that no amount of money can remove? If we don't have any answers outside our own sphere of influence, then we are truly at the mercy of whatever comes our way.

Job lost everything in a single day through unrelated tragedies. The author recorded that Job's seven sons and three daughters were feasting, drinking wine, and celebrating at the time of their deaths, which further contributes to the horrid contrast Job experienced. It's as if to say, "Job, your kids were at the peak of life, and now they are dead."

Job's entire body broke out in boils. The combination of grief, shock, and physical affliction took such a toll on Job that his closest friends could not recognize him.

It's here that we can learn something very important. During his crises, Job didn't retouch the painting. He didn't remove the shadows. Instead, he sat on the ground for seven days without uttering a word. When he finally spoke, he didn't speak in clichés. He didn't use words that we associate with hope. He wished he had never been born. He wished he would just die.

Job said:

I don't have the strength to endure. I have nothing to live for. Do I have the strength of a stone? Is my body made of bronze? No, I am utterly helpless, without any chance of success.

Job 6:11–13 NLT

34

Job wasn't a fake optimist we can't relate to. He was devastated to the point of wanting to die. His friends gave him poor advice that was full of platitudes, saying he should trust God more and he should be stronger. His friends said it was actually good for him to fall because he must have offended God.

Through Job, we are presented with the idea of universal human suffering. One of the most important things to understand about this ancient story is that he is described as being blameless. The writer of Job's life story starts by describing the high level of moral integrity he had.

Job lived an exemplary life. Morally, spiritually, ethically—he was more than just a good person. It was hard to find any character flaw! This is significant; it sets a baseline for the entire story of his life. Job had one of the most dramatic and catastrophic falls imaginable, but he did nothing to cause it. This fact removes our ability to blame Job for his problems because he was a genuinely good person to whom bad things happened. He didn't deserve the cards he was dealt. He was a victim.

On the one hand, this makes our understanding of pain more difficult. We can't use platitudes and point to a simplistic list of reasons why Job was devastated. But, on the other hand, it offers us a hand of grace. Adversity in life is not necessarily due to anything we have done to cause it. And that is our human nature. We want to know why. We want to trace clear lines of cause and effect. Like Job, though, we may never find an emotionally satisfying explanation for why suffering exists.

Yes, I know Job went on to have remarkable faith. But let's not play the faith card too quickly and rob the man of his humanity. In the same way, we should not think that even the strongest faith will prevent us from enduring such challenges—and, in fact, if we wield faith in too much of a defensive manner, we may rob ourselves of the healing and hope that comes through the process of leaning into the shadows of life when they creep our way.

What do we do with unmet expectations? The collage of all the little goals and dreams and ideas of the way our life should be, but isn't? Significant. Successful. Healthy. Influential. What happens when the picture we imagined contrasts with the reality of our lives?

I recently spoke to a man who had spent twenty-three years building a business for his family, only to lose everything when his business partner betrayed him. The liquidators came and took it all. He found himself sitting in an empty apartment with dirty blinds. He wondered if he could ever rebuild. This man was not alone in his plight. We all have to contend with shattered dreams.

We celebrate the mountaintop experiences of life. New jobs. New cars. Weddings. Anniversaries. Promotions. But real life is not only when we are at our best but also when we are experiencing trials. Lots of people know my biggest achievements—my accomplishments, my successes, my wins—but only those I trust the most know the real me. And the *real* me is the one with scars, failures, and disappointments.

Perhaps we are more our valleys than our mountains. We are our pain. We are our battles. When you know those parts of who I am, you know the soul of my life. When I see the perfect version of someone's life, I know I am seeing only a veneer. But when I know their pain, I know the real person.

If you are walking through a valley, I want you to know that I am your advocate. I'm walking alongside you. I'm asking some of the same questions as you. I can't promise you a silver bullet. I can't erase your adversity with a simple answer. Rather, I write from the place you are in right now, and I ask you to give me the privilege of taking you on a journey that will give you a framework for seeing your life in a whole new light. It may even give you the fortitude to take another step and keep looking forward.

Put simply, don't sanitize your mess.

Be real, be authentic, and allow yourself to be human. We want to see the age, the weathering, the scars of life. We don't need a masterpiece of neon colors: we want the original, vintage truth, like the original da Vinci masterpiece. Show your story. Don't hide it. Don't be embarrassed by it. Don't gloss it up. *Own it.*

> When I see the perfect version of someone's life, I know I am seeing only a veneer. But when I know their pain, I know the real person.

If we are not honest about our hurt, we will never be able to process pain in a healthy way. We build walls, even to keep out those we love. We react and attack others. We continue cycles of dysfunction. We live haunted by the expectation that people will let us down.

There is strength and power in saying, "This is me." I'm in debt. I just received a life-threatening diagnosis. I have an estranged family member. I suffer from depression. The broken parts of you are not a lesser version of yourself—they make up the authentic version of you.

Cliché hope

I have had doubts about what many have come to believe about hope. These doubts grew as I saw good people—people of integrity, faith, and optimism—go through storms like cancer, death, and family breakdowns.

There is no immunity to pain.

There is an impostor version of hope, though, that is like a promotional brochure advertising a product that doesn't work. It's the *Saint Anne* restoration all over again. It's the removal of shadows from the story of our lives. I want to give it a label: cliché hope.

Cliché hope is the promise of a pain-free life. It's the theory that if you live a certain way or follow certain principles, you can somehow avoid crises, bad circumstances, and storms. You can have the postcard family, house, and car of your dreams. That's what Job's friends thought. And it is also why they handled his crises so poorly.

Do we really buy into the idea that we can somehow "succeed" ourselves out of pain?

More money.

More connections with powerful people.

More influence.

More knowledge.

Can any of these things really save us from the troubles of life?

The obvious question is, Can I avoid pain?

However, the more important question is, Should I avoid pain?

Not the kind of pain that we would willingly inflict on ourselves through some kind of masochistic mentality. No,

I'm talking about the reality of life—that with sun comes storms. With summer comes winter. With day comes night. With hills come valleys.

I have an exercise for you. Take a pen and a blank piece of paper. If you don't have access to that right now, your imagination will suffice. On that piece of paper, sketch a line that represents your personal growth over the years of your life.

The chances are it would not be a totally straight line. Why? Because personal growth does not happen in a consistent, predictable curve. It's not a line with an even gradient.

If we charted our growth, we would see peaks and troughs. We would see plateaus and breakthroughs. We may even see a mix of incoherent circles and sharp lines.

> **The more important question is, Should I avoid pain?**

We would see times when everything is flat. We felt stuck. In a rut. Discouraged. It seemed like we were going nowhere at work. Finishing our degree seemed like an eternity away. Our dreams so distant on the horizon. Putting in effort and not getting results.

We would then see times where our growth spiked *dramatically*. It surged uphill on the chart.

What triggers growth in our character, in our identity, in our confidence, in our story?

Typically, it is the crucibles of life.

These defining challenges are catalysts that cause our growth to soar. Chances are, your times of greatest personal growth were not while lying by the pool at a resort. Or on a cruise. Or at the easiest, most pleasant times of your life.

When we understand the good that adversity brings us, it causes us to lean into the difficulties of life. Often, the things we most wished away had within them a gift—a gift to grow us. It is not the easy things that grow us! So, if you are going through crises, hardship, or delays, chances are you are growing. Look for circles and plateaus. Embrace the twists. Don't look for straight lines.

If we pursue the artificial path of cliché hope, we will try to go around things we are supposed to go through. But eventually, like Job, we will all go through seasons that money can't fix. And if the idea of true, unstoppable hope—that pain is not our end—appears nowhere in our mix of personal values and beliefs, then we will lack the tools to process the shadows of life.

It's not problems that trap us. It's how we respond to problems that becomes the much greater problem.

Cliché hope is not helpful. Cliché hope can, in fact, be insulting. It can be insulting to the parent who has lost a baby, to the teenager who has been bullied at school, and to the middle-aged person fighting discouragement so severe that suicidal thoughts are never far from their mind.

Remember, the force of hope starts at the point of your deepest need, but it doesn't ignore or diminish this need. We need to abandon the veneer that we've built around the idea that our lives will always be happy and problem free.

Has the concept of hope been photocopied so many times that it has lost its original legibility? I am personally fatigued with cliché hope slogans such as "Just think positively, and things will turn out fine," or the belief that if our hope is deep enough or spiritual enough, it can somehow bleach the pain from our lives.

My theory is that this raw version of hope—the one that springs from need—is, in fact, more helpful, more useful, and more powerful than cliché hope.

The beauty of flawed hope

When I set out to write about pain and hope, I didn't want to look at it from an aerial-view perspective, with lofty vocabulary, soaring quotes, and inspiring rhetoric. I wanted to do something different and address this subject from where we live: from a street view.

We must wrestle with the tensions of pain and hope in homes, in relationships, in marriages, in our communities. This will be gritty and have some texture. For me, the aerial view can be so far detached from real life that it doesn't really help when it comes to tangible trials and storms.

I also want to steer away from outcome-based hope that is reliant on our circumstances resolving perfectly. Outcome-based hope is a faulty idea that has no foundation in reality. Its structural integrity is about as robust as a house of cards: one bump away from collapse.

One typical way of telling Job's story is to say a man lost everything, had hope, and got back even more than he lost. I've come to resist this version of the story, though.

It strikes me as almost callous to consider *that* as a story of victorious recovery. After all, what can replace the loss of ten children? *Newer* children? To anyone who has experienced the loss of a loved one, especially a child, this rings hollow. It is recovery only to a degree. Yes, Job moved on. He rebuilt his family and business, and the second half of his life was even more successful than the first (see Job 42:12–13). But it would be devastating for any of us to go through the same trauma and sequence of events.

His children never came back to life. Job did *not* recover what mattered most in his life.

It may be uncomfortable to see the unresolved pain in this story, but it brings us right to the heart of hope—even in pain and despair, hope flourishes.

Job's story is uglier than we give it credit for. It is also more layered. His faith deepened, his purpose was forged, he rebuilt his family and business, and his life echoes all these generations later as an inspiration to us all. Think of all the things the tragedy never took from Job: his faith, his purpose, his potential, and his legacy. Those, in themselves, make a beautiful story. As we will discover, Job's life only makes sense from an eternal perspective.

With Job, I could not wrap the ribbon around the box and present a neatly finished package. The *hope* that Job truly discovered must be more than "he got things back after he lost them." What was it that Job discovered that enabled him to thrive through pain? And what can we learn from it for our modern-day lives?

A hope that is anchored to getting everything back, finishing with more money, or seeing bad circumstances become good is fragile. We would need to package it with caution tape and label it *Handle with Care*. That sort of hope could not survive the rigors of a real-life storm, where circumstances don't always resolve themselves.

Perhaps it's convenient for us to celebrate the "before and after" photos of Job's life. But what would have happened if Job were too old to have kids again or never recovered financially? Would cracks appear in that species of hope?

What if Job's hope was the opposite of what we often celebrate? What if his hope had nothing to do with outcomes, and everything to do with whom he trusted?

Cliché hope is only loud when it sees desired outcomes and often sulks quietly in the corner when things don't happen as planned. We need hope to be our loyal companion and a steady voice of support, regardless of the circumstances.

Is that not the very nature of hope?

A hope that is anchored to getting everything back, finishing with more money, or seeing bad circumstances become good is fragile.

Our lives are not neatly packaged. They are complex. They are not sterile laboratories. Life is messy. It traverses both breathtaking summits and gut-wrenching valleys. If everything always ends up perfect, then we don't need hope. Hope is there precisely because things won't always unfold in the manner we want them to. Hope is our guide, our anchor, our oxygen. This kind of hope enables us not merely to survive trials but to extract lessons from them, which, in turn, allows us to grow and become better people.

I recently found a photo of myself from many years ago. In an instant, I felt myself travel back in time.

A thought abruptly crossed my mind: if only I could go back to that season and undo all the mistakes I would make over the next ten years.

Now, logically, in that ten-year period I had a lot of wins, a lot of progress, a lot of highlights. And yet, the thought was there. I not only thought about the desire to undo mistakes, I felt it—I felt *regret*. I felt embarrassment. I felt foolish for not knowing better or doing better. Have you ever felt this kind of regret?

The cold reality is this—none of us can travel even a second back in time to undo things. The past truly is over. A bigger reality is this—we all learn from our mistakes. It's how we grow. And, typically, people who make a lot of mistakes are doing a lot of living! We make mistakes, but we never *are* a mistake.

Wishing to remove the blemishes from the canvas of our lives is a trap. It's a trap not because it is impossible, but because the lessons we learned from those situations have likely become the pillars we have built our lives on.

Some of my worst moments were what pushed me toward empathy, kindness, humility, and a reliance on the grace of God. Whatever I thought my mistakes would steal from me, they have given me much more in return.

There will always be blotches of mud on the postcard picture we thought our lives were going to be. What do we do when the life we thought we were going to live didn't happen as we planned? If only I could scrub that stain out—the regret, the mess-up, the mistake, the hurt. But it has now become a part of the story of my life. I can't erase it.

Our mistakes don't define our story. They are a part of the plot that gets woven into our story line. But with hope, our story line always curves toward a redemptive purpose.

Someone decided that Leonardo da Vinci's masterpiece needed to be enhanced and brightened, and we can make the same mistake with the challenges in our lives. But before Job started to think about restoration and future possibility, he sat amid the ashes of his life and absorbed them into his soul. While it's hard to reveal imperfections, hope starts with honesty. Don't put chemicals on the canvas of your life to polish it and brighten the colors. Shadows provide depth.

It is not hope that is the problem, but the brand of cliché hope that has become the mass-market norm. I think that in many ways, I am on a campaign against this brand of hope that is too photogenic and tidy. It's hard to find true hope when we are exhausting our energies on image creation.

So, be the broken you. Be the flawed you. Be the imperfect you. Hope's light shines through the brokenness. It's the cracks that let the light in.

God whispers to us in our pleasures, speaks in our conscience, but shouts in our pain.

—C. S. Lewis[1]

CHAPTER 3

Eucatastrophe

The greatest good comes from greatest pain

HE SMOKED A PIPE, preferred to ride his bicycle instead of driving a car, and once came to a party dressed in a polar bear costume. When dating his future wife, he would sit on the balcony of a café and drop lumps of sugar into the hats of unsuspecting passersby.

J. R. R. Tolkien was an enthralling person.

Although Tolkien was a literary giant of the twentieth century, writing books was really more of a side hobby for him (as was inventing his own languages). His day job was as a professor at the University of Oxford. In addition to the numerous languages he invented from scratch, Tolkien was fluent in Latin, French, German, Finnish, Greek, and Italian! Even today, his signature works, such as *The Lord of the Rings* and *The Hobbit*, are loved around the world.

Tolkien, however, was no stranger to pain. His father died of rheumatic fever when he was three years old. Later in life, when grieving the death of his closest friend, C. S. Lewis, Tolkien wrote in a letter to his daughter, "So far I have felt . . . like an old tree that is losing all its leaves one by one: this feels like an axe-blow near the roots."[2]

In his early twenties, Tolkien enlisted to serve in World War I. In the Battle of the Somme, he experienced some of the most brutal and bloody trench fighting of the war. His fellow soldiers were gunned down at an alarming rate, and the likelihood of survival was slim.

But one small detail during the experience changed not only the course of Tolkien's life but also the course of twentieth-century literature: Tolkien contracted a debilitating fever. On November 8, 1916, he was sent back to England. Tolkien later said that all but one of his dearest friends from school were killed in the war. Tolkien, however, was saved.

I wonder if Tolkien was conscious of this small but significant turn in his story when he coined the term *eucatastrophe*. It was, after all, not a promotion, an inheritance, or a victory that spared his life. It was a serious sickness. If it were not for this affliction, we would, in all likelihood, never have been graced by some of the most beloved literary works of the twentieth century.

I spent many months searching for a word that shows how good can come from pain. When I couldn't find an English word, I turned to Spanish, Greek, Latin . . . and no matter how many dictionaries I combed through, I couldn't quite find a word with the sense of tension I was looking for. I decided to look back in time, and it was there, in the writings of Tolkien, that I came across a word that to me is extremely special. It's unique because Tolkien had to create the word to describe what he saw as central to the story of life.

Why is it so hard to find an English word that shows how good can come from our pain? Does it surprise you that I had to reach back into the twentieth century to find a word that comes from a generation that knew immense adversity in order to help us develop a modern vocabulary for hope? It furthers the point that in our world today, we fundamentally see adversity as the enemy to our happiness—and it's this notion that needs correcting.

Eucatastrophe is a compounding of the word *catastrophe* with the Greek prefix *eu*, meaning good. A good catastrophe? I'm drawn to the abruptness of this word. It's confrontational. After all, the words *good* and *catastrophe* are seldom put together, being on opposing ends of the human experience. It's like two archnemeses joining forces—there's a tension.

It was in his essay "On Fairy-Stories"[3] that Tolkien first used the term,[4] and in 1944 he wrote to his son, "I coined the word 'eucatastrophe': the sudden happy turn in a story which pierces you with a joy that brings tears."[5] Tolkien had indeed captured a great degree of thought and meaning in that one word.

> **Eucatastrophe is a compounding of the word catastrophe with the Greek prefix eu, meaning good.**

Think about it—a fever (something bad) preserved Tolkien's life (something good). The debilitating fever had him removed from the battlefield, where the lives of many of his comrades ended. So, through the rearview mirror of history, we can now say that this sickness provided a turn toward a greater future and a broader good. It is plausible that the fever was the mechanism that saved Tolkien's life and allowed his gift of writing to be unleashed on generations to come. This reminds me of Steve Jobs (the founder of Apple), who said this in a commencement speech at Stanford University: "You can't connect the dots looking forward; you can only connect them looking backward. So you have to trust that the dots will somehow connect in your future."[6]

I'm certainly not for one moment suggesting that every tragedy, loss, failure, hurt, or pain is good in and of itself. But is it possible that, in the darkest moments of life, the green sprouts of new life and growth can develop? Isn't that the whole idea of hope? That when life hits its lowest point, this special gift of hope emerges in its most potent form, enabling us to lift our eyes once more to the horizon?

Tolkien was describing the version of hope I am talking about—at the point of deepest pain is the start of the greatest good.

People have long foraged for words that capture the idea that hope and adversity are not only connected but intrinsically reliant on each other. Beauty from ashes, light at the end of the tunnel, the sun after a storm. The awareness of a hidden link between our difficulties in life and our destiny is not new. Perhaps we don't realize the strength of this union. Perhaps understanding the marriage between life's challenges and our potential is one of the great keys to human growth and achievement.

The *idea* of hope looks nice on Hallmark cards and inspiring quotes on social media, but when we experience hardship in our lives, we need more than slogans and platitudes.

In contemporary thought, the idea of hope is often diluted by the false promise that we can live a trouble-free life, exempt from hardship and crises. Yet, generations before us would attest that it was these very trials and challenges that forged greatness in them. It is this same virtue that is found in the stories of the most innovative companies, celebrated athletes, and high achievers throughout history. Hardship and hope *together* can do something for us that a problem-free life never could.

Pain and promise

Pain is fascinating in its behavior. Pain management at the physical level has become its own area of medical expertise. People who manage their back pain, arthritis, and other ailments spend billions every year on pharmaceuticals.

But pain of the soul is much harder to study or remedy. You can't put it under a microscope. Sometimes, it is hard to define its origin.

We often see pain and hope as having irreconcilable differences.

But I'm discovering that life is more like a bicycle. Every time you get on a bicycle and ride, both wheels are in motion. The similarity is this: instead of there being seasons where there is only good in our lives and other seasons where there is only bad, we tend to have a mixture of both. We travel on both wheels at all times. Even on the most dramatically good days, we have hardships. And on the worst of days, there is some good. There is the wheel of human experience that involves hurt, pain, and hardship. But there is also the divine wheel that involves hope, peace, and joy. Any journey involves both wheels constantly in motion.

Let me tease this out a little.

I lost my job but went home to a wife who loves me.

My business just earned its biggest profits. I sprained my ankle playing a sport.

There are unexpected challenges with my kids, but I got a major win with the project I just finished at work.

My friend of twenty-three years betrayed me. The scans of my lungs are clear.

I bought my first house, but my mental health is spiraling.

For years, I bought into the popular idea that the seasons of life come in immaculate categories. I'd delay my sense of joy until the problems in my life vanished. I was waiting for some mythical day when I could finally go to sleep at night and have no challenges, pain, or problems. But if we do this, we may be waiting forever before we truly embrace the happiness available to us right now. Experiencing joy is not reliant on your life being free from every discomfort. Don't delay permitting yourself to fully embrace joy by waiting for some undefined day in the future. Seize it today, right now, in the middle of the mess you are in.

Life is an alloy, and the mixture of hardship and hope makes us stronger.

Isn't that what we often think hope is—hoping for a future day when all hardship is eliminated? But chances are high (amazingly high) that we will always experience a certain number of imperfections every day of our lives. This is what hope is for. In the present. In the pain. In the storm. It doesn't just look forward to a better day—instead, it tells us that we can make it through *this* day. Life is an alloy, and the mixture of hardship and hope makes us stronger.

I've had to interrogate my worldview so I can better understand the nature of both pain and hope. I am learning that we need to be able to see, feel, and relate to the full spectrum of human experience—because that is *our* experience. Our worldview needs to stretch into the shadows to include pain, suffering, and hardship.

We have to be able to hold both pain and promise. True hope is robust enough to allow us to ride on both wheels.

Symbiosis

A eucatastrophe can wrap its fingers around pain in one hand and grasp hold of potential in the other, wrestling the two together. That's where the magic is. Hope has a symbiotic relationship with hardship. The better we can learn this, the more likely we are to prevent fear, pessimism, and a sense of helplessness from taking over our minds.

Surprisingly and counterintuitively, real hope is found only at the center of life's challenges. A conversation on hope only exists if the voices of crises and challenges have a seat at the same table. In fact, when Job was going through the agony of losing his family and wealth, he likened his life to gold being refined and purified in a furnace, for fire does not destroy the gold—it reveals the value (Job 23:10). Job saw this as a picture of the eucatastrophe he was experiencing. Hope and adversity may seem like enemies, but they are part of the same family tree. They are genetically related. To see our troubles within the broader context of new growth is a game changer.

We often view hope and pain at opposite ends of the human spectrum—much in the same vein as we do faith and doubt. I've discovered that faith and doubt are not polar opposites but rather close relatives. Similarly, it is the existence of pain that allows hope to express itself. Hope lives in the presence, not the absence, of suffering and crises. So, even when you feel hopeless, you are closer to the life-saving virtue of hope than you realize. Growth and pain often have the same street address.

I love the writings of James in the New Testament. His letter reads,

When troubles of any kind come your way, consider it an opportunity for great joy. For you know that when your faith is tested, your endurance has a chance to grow. So let it grow, for when your endurance is fully developed, you will be perfect and complete, needing nothing.

James 1:2–4

James and Tolkien are saying the same thing. Tolkien calls it a eucatastrophe—a good tragedy—and James says troubles are an opportunity for great joy because they enable us to grow. What did James understand about troubles that made him consider them opportunities that should be celebrated? Maybe he knew that the greatest challenges bring the greatest growth.

Museum of Failure

The Museum of Failure is unlike any other collection in the world. Instead of showcasing iconic masterpieces or rare historical artifacts, it focuses on the role that failures play in great innovations. The museum's exhibits include more than a hundred of what it calls "epic fails." For example, when Colgate made a beef lasagna toothpaste, or when Heinz made purple-colored ketchup. The purpose behind the museum is not to mock past failures but to showcase how failed products and ideas were part of the stories behind successful companies.

This study of failed products and ideas clearly shows that they were actually helpful. These failures were catastrophes at the time, but in the grander scheme of things they were iterations that paved the way to success. In other words, great successes normally arise out of the ashes of spectacular failures. Even in business, then, we see the dynamic of eucatastrophes. Some of the most prominent companies in the world achieved their success through the path of pain.

In the human experience, the path is the same: adversity is the ecosystem for new growth and purpose. Stand-up comedian Jerry Seinfeld spoke about his own life journey: "If I had to trade in the experiences I've had in my life, the last ones I'd trade in would be the really bad ones. Those are the things I'd hold on to until the end, because those are the ones that harden your resolve."[7]

> **We need to reframe how we view our troubles.**

Some of your greatest good will come *because* of pain, setbacks, and disappointments—not in spite of them. How many of our opportunities are like Tolkien's fever in World War I? We need to reframe how we view our troubles.

Tolkien said that good and pain can live together in the same word, and joy and tears can occur at the same point in a story. James said that we can harness troubles as opportunities for growth and learn to celebrate them. Our problems today may look like a dead stump, or even purple ketchup, but it's from this very state that the new version of ourselves will emerge.

Pain is the antagonist in the script of our life. It provokes an accelerated growth response in our lives like nothing else can. Some of the greatest challenges we experience in life will also turn out to be the best sources of opportunity, renewal, and creativity. Our greatest challenges in life are linked to our greatest growth.

There are moments when I wish I could roll back the clock and take all the sadness away, but I have the feeling that if I did, the joy would be gone as well.

—Nicholas Sparks[1]

CHAPTER 4

Backyard Basketball

Embrace everyday moments

I GREW UP PLAYING BASKETBALL. I still remember riding my bicycle to the local neighborhood court to play with other kids. In the NBA, basketball is a study of sophisticated analytics and statistics. The most basic statistic of a basketball game is this: the farther from the hoop a player is when they shoot, the lower their rate of success. In fact, you are rewarded with an extra point if you make a shot from beyond the three-point line. It might seem out of place to be talking about basketball in a book about hope, but I want to intentionally steer the conversation toward some practical examples we encounter in our everyday lives.

The game of basketball has been revolutionized by a player named Stephen Curry. His long-range shooting is extremely efficient, and he has smashed individual records and won multiple NBA championships. What is fascinating about Stephen Curry is how he developed into such a prodigious player.

Before becoming a breakout superstar, Stephen was overlooked by many talent scouts. One said, "His first step is average at best, and considering his skinny frame and poor explosiveness around the basket in traffic, it's unlikely that he'll be able to get to the free throw line anywhere near as much in the NBA as he does in college."[2] Others said he was too slow and too small. So, how did such an unlikely athlete not only make it to the NBA, but also become such a success that he changed the entire league?

The answer may surprise you. I had to go back two generations to Stephen's grandfather, who built a backyard basketball court for his family. Whenever Stephen visited, he would practice for long hours on that court. The makeshift basket was attached to a light pole and a flimsy fiberglass board. The ground was uneven, with rocks and mud providing obstacles for the ball—a far cry from the polished hardwood and glass backboards of the NBA.[3] To avoid having to constantly chase the ball as it bounced away on the rocky ground, every shot had to be precisely on target. It wasn't pretty, but the obstacles actually provided an incentive to be accurate and consistent—shoot well and chase the ball less. This subpar basketball system became the context that helped develop the most successful sharpshooter in the history of basketball.

In other words, the everyday challenges of Stephen's context were what made him great. Playing on an amateur backyard court was a disadvantage, and the only way to reduce the chance of the ball bouncing away was to shoot more accurately. Out of a daily challenge came something even greater. Perhaps, in his imagination, Stephen Curry also envisioned a grander venue than the homemade basketball court: he dreamed of one day playing in the best arenas in the world.

What we initially consider as inconveniences or hardships can later be celebrated as the tools that developed us. We can also apply these same concepts to Job: the very crises that threatened to destroy his life forged him into the leader we are still learning from, thousands of years later.

Everyday hope

Developing hope when we face small challenges in life prepares us for the larger storms. It's a misunderstanding to think that hope is reserved for only the obvious and ominous crises of life. Hope is not just seen in the glaring spotlight of life's major disasters; it's revealed in the dim candle flicker of everyday moments. Our daily attitude, perspectives, and approaches to people ultimately construct the true center stage.

> **Hope is not just seen in the glaring spotlight of life's major disasters; it's revealed in the dim candle flicker of everyday moments.**

It is too easy to become accustomed to the subtle forms of despair that grip us daily. Raising children, managing household finances, coping with the demands of a busy career—all of us face the burden of these kinds of pressures. We also need to find hope in these moments.

The idea of suffering and troubles does not only refer to life's major crises. It also speaks to the degree of stress we all carry with us, whether it be through daily anxieties, chronic health issues, disappointments, or relationship struggles. The anxiety could come from something routine, like a looming deadline, or something more emotional, such as a growing sense that your dream is floating away, forever out of reach. All the little daily difficulties in life eventually add up to a tally that's much higher than one-off, stand-alone storms. If hope matters, it matters this very instant, regardless of the degree of difficulty we might currently face.

Pain hides

Sometimes, the gnawing challenges we face are more subliminal than an obvious catastrophe. No car accident. No funeral. No bankruptcy. For example, when a sudden problem hits, we can often put a specific time and date in our journal, marking the exact instant when things changed. But what about more gradual weights on the soul? When does loneliness start? When does depression begin? When is the genesis of feeling like our life is purposeless?

Don't be fooled. These more gradual sorrows cause as much damage as the tornado; they just do so with less dramatic effect. They act like a "hopelessness funnel" into which we slip further and further and can't seem to climb our way out.

Pain hides. One of the behaviors of pain that has surprised me the most is how stealthy it can be. It accumulates in secret. I remember reaching a point in my life when I realized I had become emotionally fragmented. Since my early twenties, my life has accelerated at a rapid pace. Moving internationally twice. Pioneering businesses and a nonprofit. Raising three sons. Studying at multiple colleges and universities. I sat down, reviewed the last twenty years of my life, and found that, from the time I finished high school, I had been pushing and building—and at some point, it all caught up with me.

If you had asked me before this season, I would have told you that pain and trauma are identifiable events. I didn't comprehend that this wasn't the only way pain behaved—that it can accumulate like grains of sand, and over time, your soul can feel suffocated by it.

For me, it wasn't one particular event. One day, I awoke in a mist, and I began to feel less energized and without vision.

As gradual as it is, it is also sudden. And it's stubborn.

When pain arrived, I almost felt like I wasn't quite the person I used to be. A spark was missing. Perhaps for me it was as if I had hoarded all the trials, challenges, failures, and discouragement without ever realizing it. And, in one fell swoop, pain decided to announce itself. In that moment, it was daunting because I finally saw it and I realized, "Oh, no, it's all here within me." Ignoring it didn't cause it to go away. Instead, it found parsonage in my soul.

I learned this: pain accumulates. It can be people pain, failure pain, discouragement pain, and so on. But know this: pain doesn't go away without us engaging with it or processing it in a healthy way. I decided the "mist" was not something to ignore but to explore. On a long road trip through the Rocky Mountains of Colorado, I saw a picture of my life. The mountains had sheer rock faces that soared to the heavens. It made the valley road feel as if it was almost being swallowed up. It was impossible to see the horizon or get any kind of picture of what was ahead. I knew that internally I was in an emotional valley. But when we embrace the road through the valley, and its depths and shadows, something new eventually opens up. Ultimately, valleys are passageways. Something new is on the other side.

Valleys are not our enemy. Sometimes, they are places where we do necessary soul work. Even though those seasons can feel dark and confusing, there is always a new chapter just ahead. This was the case in my journey through that chapter of my life.

In high school, I remember having to swim four lengths of the pool fully clothed as part of a life-saving course. Upon entering the water, it didn't seem too bad: I could still kick. Still throw one arm over the other. But gradually, the wet clothes became a weighty anchor. After a few minutes, I imagined how someone thrown overboard in the high seas might feel. Was it possible they would get to the point where the weight and burden they were carrying would drag them under?

That simulation taught me a lot about the difficulties of rescuing a drowning person. But now, as I reflect on it, I think of the weight many people carry through their lives every day. Every stroke of the arm is laborious. Chronic stress may not have a definitive starting point, but it is something we can carry within us for years. We are swimming, but it feels like all our effort goes into just keeping our heads above water. Racing? Winning? No—these ideas are a luxury we gave up a long time ago.

The subtle day-to-day weights that we carry can have an even greater impact than a more noticeable dramatic and painful event. But this low-grade fever of the soul can be hard to identify, because we can't peg it to some kind of major tragedy that has occurred. The everyday challenges that we carry can take a significant toll on our mental health and inner vitality.

The ongoing challenges that affect our emotions are constant weights that burden us every day. They are as worthy adversaries as the sudden crisis that strikes with lightning and thunder. Loneliness on a crowded planet is an example of the kind of weight we sometimes swim with every day. Perhaps the effect of loneliness has been amplified through the social media revolution—we are surrounded by a shadow of friendship but rarely get to sit in its actual sunlight.

Followers. Friends. Photos. Videos. Views. Likes. But, at the end of the day, none of it has warmth, a hand to hold when watching a movie, a shoulder to lean on during a difficult moment, a friend to laugh with over coffee, a family to love unconditionally. To be alone, among the billions of others on this planet, can be devastating. This is just one of the many inner challenges that can erode our hope for the future.

On my own journey, I have often downgraded the importance of the daily routine of life and over-elevated the importance of milestone moments. For example, as a father of three sons, what truly matters is not just the birthdays, graduations, and major achievements: I need to see the more important value in the daily conversations we have at dinnertime, the joy of throwing a ball in the afternoon sun, and the routine of normal home life.

Hope matters at the grocery store. It matters as you sit at your desk at work. It can help you in the everyday moments of life. We need to place hope on a low-enough shelf that it is accessible at all times.

Perhaps hope on a daily level is, in some ways, a rehearsal for the big moments in life. What if hope were like a muscle, built through the tearing and rebuilding of the everyday grind, so that one day, when we're in need of great strength, we could find it there? Any musician will say the same thing: the grand performance is made possible only by the years of daily practice.

Nea Ionia

When you have a challenge you can't change, embrace it. A perfect example of this is my grandmother, who is affectionately known as Lula. A very short Greek lady. Dark, curly hair. Olive skin. She cooks the best lasagna I've ever tasted. She is the happiest person I know. I assumed that her journey through life had been relatively smooth since she constantly laughs and has such a positive nature. However, I recently discovered some facts about my grandmother's life that shocked me tremendously.

When you have a challenge you can't change, embrace it.

In the 1940s, she lived in a small town called Nea Ionia, outside of Athens, at a time when Greece was being invaded by the Germans and Italians. The men dug rudimentary tunnels in their backyards as a form of protection from German bombs. Lula told me that whenever she hears a siren, she is reminded of running into these underground tunnels as a child. It was a remarkable and horrendous chapter of world history.

Lula also told me about an event that occurred when she was eleven years old. She went to see a movie in an open-air theater with her brother. Just as the movie began, it stopped, and the lights came on. Uniformed Gestapo soldiers with rifles walked down the aisles, shouting for everyone to stand. Even at her tender age, Lula knew anything could happen. She and her brother quietly clung to each other as they were marched out into the public square. It was just soil. No grass. The soldiers separated the women and children from the men and lined all of the men up.

The next thing my grandmother remembers is the crack of the rifles and the smell of gunpowder as the men were massacred in front of her eyes.

My grandmother went through immense trauma and pain. A world war. A divorce. Immigrating and starting a new life in a foreign culture. When I quizzed her on how she had developed such a joyful and optimistic demeanor in life, she could not point to any one mega-decision that changed everything. Rather, she told me about the daily choice she makes: to focus on helping others. The joy in being with children. Her love of olive oil, lemons, garlic, and Greek salads. She embraces everyday moments.

Her path was not without resistance and great hardship, yet that same path is what made her who she is. I reference the story of my grandmother because it is a striking contrast to our modern idea of happiness—lives without trouble and pain. I am able to compare my life's troubles to hers and get a quick perspective check on how insignificant my issues are. But, more than that, I see a way of thinking that some people from generations before us seemed to innately understand—that hope and hardship are not opposites; they are related in a way that we must understand in order to truly flourish in life. This concept teaches us that ideas and virtues eventually have to be expressed in our everyday lives. They must color the way we talk and affect our actions. A virtue must, therefore, become a daily habit. The big idea in the cloud must be brought down to a granular level.

Hope needs to be more than an idea: it must move us to act. And the little actions of joy—things that feel seemingly insignificant in light of all the grandeur, rhetoric, and quotes about hope—are not so little after all. Choosing to get out of the house and walk the dog, choosing to apply for a new job, choosing to spot new potential and opportunities while still in the midst of your problems—these everyday choices matter. In fact, for the most part, it is helpful to avoid seeing hope as one dramatic decision you make, but rather as the multiplied effect of many very small, individual everyday choices.

I may not know what tomorrow holds, but *right now* I can choose to smile. *Right now* I can choose to be kind to those around me. I can do the next thing, and by doing the next thing, I have taken a step forward in my journey. Hope is for now. It is for this very day. You can benefit *right now* from this energizing, life-giving virtue. Don't wait another minute to orient your perspective toward hope.

Hope is not just for dark times—it is for all times. What you expect for the future matters not only for *then*, it matters for *now*. Life is never perfect. You may be experiencing great success in one area of life—but chances are, you will be having some troubles in other areas. Don't postpone being optimistic until everything in your life feels good. Start today!

What is a challenge you are facing at this moment? So often, we resent and wish away our everyday trials. But when we take another look at those same challenges through the lens of hope, we can see more than an obstacle: we see the context for growth. Through the lens of hope, these challenges can become the very things that mold and shape our potential. Many of the greatest inventors, the most talented artists, and the most inspiring leaders can point back to a context of daily challenges that made them into something special.

Your backyard basketball court may be run down, or your schedule too full to pursue studying, or your manager may not believe in you. Instead of allowing these things to fill your mind with negativity, see them through the prism of hope. The muddy ground is refining you, though you don't realize it. The things that inconvenience you in one season can accelerate you in the next.

Believe in the best. Develop optimism. Expect good things. Choose positivity. Laugh. Dream of the brightest future you can imagine. That vision will change your life now, regardless of what happens next.

Hope cannot just be an intellectual belief, though. If it is, we often won't see the textbook definition translate to our homes, marriages, or workplaces. Hope must be emotionally absorbed. It needs to be *felt*. It needs to be expressed as a part of our personality.

We all have challenges. We need to redefine day-to-day obstacles as the friction that sharpens the blade of our destiny. Practice hope daily, and it will be there for you to call on in your crisis of the decade.

Success comes after you conquer your biggest obstacles and hurdles.

—Stephen Curry

Broken Pianos

Forge purpose from your pain

DO YOU KNOW who made the best-selling piano album of all time? The story behind it may surprise you.

In 1975, Keith Jarrett was, unwittingly, about to create history. After a long drive from Zurich, Switzerland, Jarrett finally arrived at the Cologne Opera House in Germany. He was to play the first-ever jazz concert at this venue, but he had to wait until almost midnight for his allocated time slot—all the while fighting a lack of sleep and back pain. And things were about to go from bad to worse.

Jarrett had specifically requested a Bösendorfer 290 Imperial concert grand piano for his concert. But an error was made by the staff, and a much smaller piano was placed on the stage. Some of the keys didn't play. The pedals got stuck. It was terribly out of tune. Naturally, Jarrett did not want to proceed with the concert. But, in a last-minute risk, he decided to step out in front of fourteen hundred people and play for over an hour on a broken piano.

Jarrett improvised. He changed the composition of the notes to compensate for the broken keys and thin bass register. He produced an entirely new sound—something unique, emotive, and unpredictable. The mix of his improvised and unorthodox playing, combined with the peculiar sound of the flawed piano, produced something of beauty. It has been described as revolutionary improvisation—a masterpiece.

One would imagine that the best-selling piano album of all time would have been recorded in the most acoustically refined studio, with the best piano, and the most technologically advanced microphones and equipment. Instead, it's a recording of this unusual midnight concert in Germany on a broken, undersized piano, played by a tired and annoyed artist. It went on to sell more than four million copies.

In the concert of our lives, none of us are given perfect studio conditions. We all must play with a broken piano. Some of the keys don't work. The pedals get stuck. The tuning isn't perfect. For some, that brokenness comes in the form of physical pain and disease. For others, it's heartbreak from a failed relationship, poverty, fear of the future, or family conflict. None of us gets the Bösendorfer 290 Imperial concert grand piano. Hope is having the ability to coax a masterpiece out of a damaged instrument.

Hope is having the ability to coax a masterpiece out of a damaged instrument.

Maybe the flaw in your instrument is a lack of contentment. You are caught in the comparison trap of seeing everyone else's life, and it has eroded your self-worth and belief. You are asking yourself, "What if my lucky break never comes? What if this is all there is?"

The phone call

It was a serene and peaceful afternoon when I got the call. "The test results are back. It's melanoma cancer." My older brother kept talking, telling me his test results, but I'd fallen to the ground. As I lay there feebly holding my cell phone up to my ear, the remainder of the conversation was a haze. I heard something about late-term stage four and spreading. But my heart just felt pain.

My brother had been diagnosed with a terminal, incurable cancer that would require radical treatment simply to try to prolong his life.

We grew up just eighteen months apart. BMX rides through the suburbs. Eighties music. Long school bus trips. Adventures in the backyard. Teenage years. He taught me to drive when my dad couldn't handle the stress of sitting in the passenger seat. Brothers.

The treatment. I just shake my head because it's so hard to write about. It's tough. It burns to think of what my brother had to endure. Brain radiation. Surgery. Opioids. The dark shadow of death stretched over his future. He has to wake up and hug his sons and try to find the words to describe what is happening to him. He's had to wrestle with faith and the big questions of life, not as some kind of academic debate, but as a tragic daily reality.

I include my brother's story of cancer intentionally, because, at the time of writing this chapter, five years on from that shocking diagnosis, he continues to fight for his life. It's unresolved. In the future, I hope I can report that a breakthrough medical treatment worked, or that there was a divine miracle from God. But, at this point, it remains an ongoing process.

It's the fact that my brother's diagnosis is unresolved, and without a picture-perfect ending, that I empathetically share it with you. The chances are that you are also facing challenges in your life that you can't see a way out of. It may feel like dark clouds have appeared on the horizon, and they've set in for a long, cold winter. You don't yet know how the financial stress will play out. You can't see a way out of the emotional trauma that has gripped your mental health. You are not sure if the medical treatment will work. You don't know if you can repair your marriage.

What if hope could exist within our mess? Our pain? Our reality right now? This is real-life hope. For those of us who don't have perfect lives. For those of us going through pain. For those who feel overwhelmed. It's not that I've been where you are at some past point in my life. I'm sitting with you right now, facing unresolved pain.

Something germinates in the ashes. It is kindled by the afternoon breeze. Hope sparks in the dark night of the soul. Color, beauty, and imagination are found waiting for us down the path we all scramble to escape from but can't. Walking with my brother through cancer is unresolved. Yet, he told me that he is grateful for what it has brought to his life. The suffering and pain—he said it is a gift. It's not that cancer is a gift. No. The gift is the profound inner transformation he has endured—one so rich and valuable that it has completely changed his vantage point on life, work, and parenting. I'm so inspired by his choice to forge purpose from pain. He is playing a beautiful song from the broken piano that life presented him.

What about you? What broken pianos are on the stage of your life? There are some practical actions we can all take to forge purpose from our pain. I want to give you two essential, must-have approaches to life so you can step up and play.

1. Focus on others.

Our deepest pain can come from people who hurt us. Whether it is a friend's betrayal, a marriage breakdown, or conflict within the family, humanity can be a source of pain. Yet, at the same time, people are also one of life's true recovery agents from hurt. Jarrett had an audience to perform for. The result is an enduring masterpiece.

Your life needs to have a sound that is heard by others. I don't think we can live selfish lives and also see hope do its full work. What gives us hope is the learned habit of taking our eyes off our problems and looking up to a world full of needs. Serve. Contribute. Give yourself to those who have greater needs than you.

There is no such thing as giving too much hope to others. Our world is in desperate need of light-bearers, of burden lifters. We live in an avalanche of 24/7 media that feeds us fear, negativity, and anger. We need more people to be fluent in the language of hope.

Before Job had his dramatic comeback, he said, "For I assisted the poor in their need and the orphans who required help. I helped those without hope, and they blessed me. And I caused the widows' hearts to sing for joy" (Job 29:12–13). At some point, Job looked up and focused on others. In fact, Job found those who had less hope and helped them. In doing so, he said it was *he* who was blessed.

Your piano may be broken, but there are people in this world who still need you to play.

2. Forge purpose from your pain.

Let me ask you a pointed question: What if your circumstances don't change? An even more difficult question to confront is this: What if your circumstances get *worse*?

Jarrett probably thought a long drive, a painful back, and a midnight time slot were the worst of his worries—until he discovered the broken piano.

79

Job would have thought his crisis was losing his business. Imagine his shock and devastation upon hearing that his wealth had also been lost. Then, on top of this, he lost all ten of his children on the same day? It's beyond words.

His circumstances got worse. Much worse.

How do we play when the piano won't be fixed in time? One of the most revitalizing, hope-building decisions you can make is to forge purpose from your pain. In her book *Bittersweet*, Susan Cain writes, "Bittersweetness shows us how to respond to pain: by acknowledging it, and attempting to turn it into art, the way the musicians do, or healing, or innovation, or anything else that nourishes the soul."[1] A purpose beyond ourselves gives us a reason to keep playing.

> One of the most revitalizing, hope-building decisions you can make is to forge purpose from your pain.

Our world is broken. Hardships arrive not only through challenges or mishaps but also from the hands of people. It's one thing to be diagnosed with an illness that is without explanation or cause. It is another thing to go through pain due to the direct actions of a person. Betrayal. Lies. Violence. Racism. When someone intentionally wrongs us, it carries an extra bite. Yet, sometimes, the very thing that can destroy you is also the thing that, when processed correctly, can strengthen you.

Purpose is not discovered; it is developed. You won't just stumble upon a purposeful life one day. You need to take the ingredients in your hands—the good and the bad—and develop purpose. Timothy Keller says it this way: "Nothing is more important than to learn how to maintain a life of purpose in the midst of painful adversity."[2] The purpose you develop must be bigger than the pain you have endured.

It's easy to focus on the darker shades of the palette of life. But do we have a full appreciation of the true beauty and majesty that life can bring? The wonder of a star-filled spring night, the feeling that comes from laughing so hard you cry, old friends, raising children, building a career, buying a puppy, making a difference in someone's life, seeing prayers answered. Forging purpose while you are suffering is a way of exploring the brighter end of the spectrum—the side of wonder, of laughter, of joy.

In my mind, I can picture Jarrett sitting behind his broken piano on a stage in front of hundreds of people. And I see myself. I see the instrument that I have been given in life. It, too, has broken keys. I see my faults, my limitations. Can I play something beautiful with *my* life when my instrument is blemished? Perhaps the flaws in my circumstances are not just problems to solve but catalysts that push me to create a better, more captivating purpose in my life.

Avoiding certain broken keys and the deficient tone of the piano encouraged Jarrett to produce a sound never heard before. It's not that Jarrett played something special *in spite* of a flawed instrument, but he created beauty *because* of it.

What do we do when all we have to play is a broken piano? Hope is about improvising in the middle of a real-life drama. It is about taking our eyes off the broken keys and focusing on the others. It is forging purpose through the pain and playing our concert to the world around us. Your piano may be broken, but sometimes the most beautiful art comes from flawed instruments.

When the winds of change blow, some people build walls and others build windmills.

—Chinese proverb

CHAPTER 6

Storms, Shipwrecks, Serpents

See beyond the storms

AS A CHILD, I loved the tropical storms that hit the East Coast of Australia. As I lay in my room, I was captivated by the pounding rain and blue flashes of lightning I saw through the window. I was excited to feel my heart jump as loud claps of thunder echoed through the house. While it was fun at the time, I've grown up to see the devastation that storms can bring. Sometimes, the vicious wind of a storm can be so extreme that it blows roofs off houses, overturns cars, and even strips the bark off trees!

In March 2022, the city of Brisbane experienced devastating floods that caused extensive damage to thousands of homes and businesses. After months of historically high rainfall, the nearby dam overflowed and the river that runs through the heart of the city broke its banks.

On the morning of the flood, my wife, Cindi, and I witnessed the power of nature in action. I remember seeing fridges, million-dollar yachts, and even entire houses being swept down the Brisbane River. A few days later, along with many other residents in my city, I helped people clean their homes. The stench of the thick mud and stale water was overpowering. Emotions were on edge as we entered homes to find everything destroyed. Televisions filled with water. Expensive artwork covered in mud. Family valuables swept away. My workplace was flooded. My brother's home went under. I heard of one person who had spent a million dollars remodeling his house only a month earlier; now it lay in ruins.

At that very moment, there was a tangible need for hope. One week earlier, life was normal, even carefree, for most. People went about their days without any thought about the state of their homes, possessions, and families—all of which seemed safe and secure. Then, a few days later, there were thousands of homeless people and billions of dollars of damage. Our city learned the hard way how quickly everything can change.

One of the most sobering moments for me was watching news footage of a man in another area of our state whose house had been inundated by intense flash flooding. The man survived, but his young son and wife had been swept to their deaths. He openly wept in front of the camera. My heart immediately broke for him.

Floods and storms don't just occur in nature. They happen in our lives. Like a natural storm, personal storms can arrive quite unexpectedly. They don't make appointments. Sometimes, they don't even show up on the radar; there are no warnings to signal their onslaught. When storms hit, the landscape of life suddenly shifts—whether we are ready or not. Like Job, every one of us has experienced situations over which we have no personal control, situations we did not expect and could not prevent.

Pain almost always arrives unexpectedly, and what is shocking is how fundamentally it can change our lives in an instant. Just ask anyone who has rushed, terrified, to an ICU ward, and they will attest to a palpable sense of dread that washes over them. We talk about sliding doors. Moments when everything changes. What we thought was our path to traverse in life is suddenly and drastically altered. We are pushed through another door that we never chose.

One of the most common things I hear when it comes to pain is "I didn't see it coming." The shock, the suddenness of it, adds to why it is so difficult to process. A single moment can drastically change our lives. It can come in the form of a midnight phone call, a single conversation, or a wilderness season of emotional distress we can't navigate out of. We call this a new normal. What was normal is no more. Now, we are trying to make sense of what our lives look like.

> **Some of your most game-changing lessons will come out of storms.**

A news journalist who spent many years reporting on tragedies wrote about the unexpected nature of suffering. She would often interview grieving family members or victims in the immediate aftermath of something terrible. Distilling her decades of talking with people going through hardship, she writes, "The day that turns a life upside down usually starts like any other. You open your eyes, swing your body out of bed, eat breakfast, get dressed and leave the house, your mind busy. As you close the front door behind you, rarely is there a tingle of unease that something is off. Later, when the story of what happened next comes to be told, it will start with the day's deceptive ordinariness, something that will now seem incredible. How could a blindside so momentous have struck on a day that began so unremarkably?"[1]

I think she is, unwittingly, describing what happened to Job perfectly. Job's day started like any other, and then he was blindsided by unthinkable loss. Storms should not define our lives, however. Rather, how we respond to storms should be the touchstone. Reinvention, ingenuity, learning, growth. Some of your most game-changing lessons will come out of storms. They will shape your character, they will grow your empathy, and they will unlock parts of your inner strength that you didn't know existed.

So, how do you find hope in storms?

Anchors

The anchor has become a popular symbol of hope. This symbol grew out of the writings of the New Testament. It was the apostle Paul who wrote, "This hope is a strong and trustworthy anchor for our souls" (Hebrews 6:19). Paul knew what it meant to go through rough seas. His choice of an anchor came from his own personal experience.

Once, while traveling by ship off the coast of Sicily, en route to mainland Italy, Paul encountered a violent storm that left his boat battered and without an anchor. Eventually, it was completely broken apart by the waves. This would have been enough to kill most travelers—and yet, miraculously, Paul washed up on the shore of a small island after holding on to timber debris. He dragged himself out of the lapping water onto the sand. But as he gathered some sticks to make a fire, he was bitten by a venomous snake (see Acts 27–28).

One would think the initial storm was bad enough, or that nearly drowning in the sea would be the end of Paul's troubles. But what truly intrigues me is the snakebite. For me, it represents the pain that comes when we think we can't take any more—the pain we never saw coming.

The snakebite was the tipping point. In my opinion, it should have been the moment when God intervened and said, "Enough." But instead, even after all Paul had endured, God allowed the snake to cause him further pain.

Paul was a remarkably transparent writer. He seemed to see no incongruence between being totally honest about his suffering and simultaneously holding on to a resilient faith.

A famous snippet from Paul's writings is in Romans 8: "All things work together for good to those who love God . . ." (v. 28 NKJV). It's crucial to remember what "all things" were. They were problems. Here are some specific pain points Paul mentions in this chapter alone:

Sufferings of this present time

Hope that doesn't see the answer

Personal weaknesses

Trouble and calamity

Death threats

Persecution that may lead to death

The "all things" were not good; they were *bad*. Paul's journey taught him that God can take the bad and orchestrate it into something good. However, it doesn't mean the bad doesn't exist. I have learned from Paul (also my middle name) that if I view my pain from a materialistic, comfortable vantage point, it will appear disastrous. But when I see it through an eternal filter, it will give me a wide enough perspective to include the multiple layers of human experience.

If our worldview is that God will protect us from loss when circumstances take a turn for the worse, we often don't know how to process it when loss does come. However, God's promise to me is that in all of my human experience, which will include pain, economic hardship, and challenges, grace is there to help me endure.

When the unexpected trials of life hit him, Paul knew how important it was to have an anchor in the storms.

Stand

The little blue Thomas the Tank Engine toy had started to fade with the warm afternoon sun. Just a lifeless toy. Worthless at a junk sale. Yet, if the house caught on fire, it would be the first thing Sophia would save. Even a momentary glance at the toy brought back the memory of her five-year-old boy begging her for it in the toy store. The smile on his face—the sound of his voice as he played with it on the wooden floorboards and narrated his imagination out loud.

It's been eight years since Sophia's son was lost to a rare form of cancer. Looking at the Thomas the Tank Engine toy brings grief to her heart. No more pitter-patter of little feet, no more morning hugs. Loss hits hard. The train is faded, but the agony remains—vivid, shiny, untouched. My heart was deeply moved by her story. Like Sophia and Job, those of us who have lost loved ones need an anchor to hold on to.

Think about an anchor: it's a heavy object that's lowered from a ship deep into the water. This iron hook grapples rocks on the floor of the ocean and holds the ship upright and steady. The anchor prevents shipwrecks by stopping the ship from moving. For a sailor caught in a storm, the most essential, life-saving instrument is an anchor.

In the same way, hope can anchor our hearts. Hope is the steadiness we crave amid a raging storm. It is something solid and strong that we can trust to keep us afloat.

One of the interesting things about an anchor is that you don't see it when it is working. It lies hidden beneath the surface. Above the ocean, the wind can be howling, the timbers creaking, the mast shaking—but all the while, there is a powerful anchor keeping the ship stable.

I recently went to a boat show. The boats came in all different shapes and sizes, but I noticed that all of the boat companies advertised the same features: the horsepower of the engine, its speed, and the distance the boat could travel. Like the boat show, our entire culture is focused on the same things: progress and speed. We want to go places. To progress. To achieve more. Anchors, however, are about the opposite. They are about limiting progress. They are about staying still.

That's one of the things I love about the metaphor of the anchor. Sometimes, life is not about making progress; it is simply about standing our ground in a storm. Holding fast amid crises is a remarkable achievement. Not every season is one of progress. Sometimes, the biggest win is merely to stay firmly in place.

When I think about the storm Job endured, it makes me appreciate that one of his greatest lessons to us was not what he did, but rather what he didn't do. Job didn't quit. He didn't give up on his future. Instead, he stood his ground. The flood swept through his life and brought with it emotional devastation. But Job had an inner anchor: he had faith in God. Job's expression of hope was to keep standing.

Grant and Glueck

Harvard University in Cambridge, Massachusetts, is world-renowned. For generations, some of the brightest minds have been educated there. Starting in 1938, Harvard University decided to conduct a longitudinal study, the Grant Study, on a group of 268 male sophomores. This study was later added to with another study beginning in the 1970s, the Glueck Study, with a cohort of 456 people from the inner city of Boston. The Glueck participants were intentionally chosen from the poorest and most disadvantaged situations. Pairing these very different cohorts together in one parallel study, the Harvard Study of Adult Development, provides a very fascinating pool of data.

Think about it—decades of studying two groups of men from vastly different backgrounds to discover the secrets of happiness and success in life.

The Harvard Study of Adult Development spans the Great Depression, the first moon landing, wars, the digital revolution, and a drastically changing world. It has involved generations of leading researchers analyzing brain scans and blood samples, as well as tracking the qualitative areas of people's lives in detail.

The researchers looked at their subjects' triumphs and failures, their careers and marriages, and the broader journeys of their lives.[2] They visited their subjects' homes and talked with them as they married, had children, grew into middle age, and entered into the latter years of their lives, grappling with age, sickness, and eventually death. Only nineteen of the original subjects were still alive at the time of writing.

What did eighty years of data reveal? Was it a person's IQ, social standing, wealth, or good looks that contributed most to happiness? Was it the people who got the smoothest run through life—the ones who avoided the most pain and suffering?

The discoveries were surprising.

Researchers found that the essential keys to happiness and success were strong relationships and community. It wasn't the amount of money, fame, or prestige someone had that determined their happiness. What distinguished people was how their relationships helped them respond to storms.

The Harvard Study of Adult Development revealed the ability to cope with the ups and downs of life is greatly determined by our community, which contributes to our long-term joy.[3] Having strong relationships in the midst of life's calamities may contribute more to your happiness than almost any other factor in your life.

Blizzards

Once, when I was due to fly out of Portland, Oregon, I awoke to the biggest snowstorm the city had seen that decade. A thick blanket of snow lay across the streets, and the skies were windy and grey. This arctic blast was so severe that I remember getting on my flight and watching the airport crew hose the wings with antifreeze fluid. I wasn't sure the plane would even be able to take off in such extreme conditions.

The pilot taxied the plane to the runway, and within a few minutes, we were soon racing down that icy asphalt at jet speed. The plane lifted and ascended into the dark clouds that covered the city. In less than a minute, we broke through the darkness and the cabin was flooded with sunlight. Squinting, I looked out the window, and all I could see was blue sky. I glanced down and, sure enough, we were *above* the storm clouds.

The contrast was striking: grey and white suddenly transformed into crystal clear blue, lit brightly by the morning sun.

Light is a synonym for hope. The psalmist David wrote, "Even the darkness will not be dark to you; the night will shine like the day, for darkness is as light to you" (Psalm 139:12 NIV). The human eye is so attuned to see light that if the earth were flat, we could detect a candle in the dark nearly twenty miles away.[4] Light always defeats darkness, in the same way that hope overpowers fear. And our souls have such a built-in anticipation of good that even a flicker of hope twenty miles away can excite us.

When we commit ourselves to seeing beyond the grey, we are able to see the sun, which was there all along.

Flying through the blizzard helped me realize that blue skies lie above the worst storms imaginable. The difference is perspective. Sometimes, seeing a situation or a relationship from a different perspective can totally change our view. What storms are you facing now? It could be a storm of personal failure or a relationship crisis that has darkened your world. Climb higher in your inner hope and see the blue sky. When we commit ourselves to seeing beyond the grey, we are able to see the sun, which was there all along.

For Job, the storm of losing everything helped him see his faith from a different perspective. Speaking to God, Job said, "I had only heard about you before, but now I have seen you with my own eyes" (Job 42:5). I think Job was saying that he had knowledge and some untested beliefs before the storm, but because of all that he went through, he now had a faith that he saw with clarity and conviction. It's one thing to know; it's another thing to see.

We have to see above the storm. Look beyond the discomfort and inconvenience. Every storm, no matter how intense and threatening, always ends. Stand firm. Don't move. The warm sun will burst through the clouds. Lean into the wind and rain. Keep walking.

Every sunrise shows me that darkness is temporary.

Every breath shows me that I still have a future.

Every heartbeat tells me to keep moving.

Having done all, stand firm.

Character cannot be developed in ease and quiet. Only through experience of trial and suffering can the soul be strengthened, vision cleared, ambition inspired, and success achieved.

—Helen Keller

Tightrope

Overcome anxiety

WHEN PEOPLE VISIT the Grand Canyon, most stand nervously at the edge, finding a way to enjoy the breathtaking view while maintaining enough distance to stay safe. But one man dreamed of attaching a two-inch cable to either side of the chasm and walking across it with nothing but a balancing stick.

Nik Wallenda is a seventh-generation tightrope walker. This activity is so inherently dangerous that some of his family members have been injured, or have even died, in accidents. His great-grandfather, the legendary Karl Wallenda, perished in a high wire attempt in Puerto Rico in 1978. The grainy video footage of him wobbling, slipping, and falling is haunting.

For more than one hundred years, the Wallenda family has upped the stakes to draw in bigger crowds. Nik, however, has undertaken the most extreme spectacles. He is the first person to walk on a wire directly over Niagara Falls, battling thick mist and wind swells.

In 2013, Nik attempted to walk across the Grand Canyon with no safety wire, no parachute, and no second chances. I joined a live global audience of nearly thirteen million people and watched with a morbid curiosity to see what would happen. The broadcasters rigged Nik with a microphone, so we could hear every word as he danced with death fifteen hundred feet above the Little Colorado River. Normally I am comforted when I hear someone pray, but hearing him plead with God to save him made me feel even more anxious. It was like listening to some kind of primal human experience.

I was sweating. My heart pounded in my chest. And I was just a guy in my living room watching it on television! Nik was buffeted by wind gusts up to forty-eight miles per hour, and the dust-covered cable was shaking underneath his feet. Every step was a force of will. This death-defying feat was full of nail-biting moments as Nik conquered his fear of death. After about a quarter of a mile tiptoeing on a cable, Nik made it safely to the other side, breaking world records and embracing his family. He showed the world that the human spirit is stronger than fear.

I was not only spellbound but also inspired by the journey of this man who could so radically conquer extreme stress. The image is striking, but it also captures life in a single frame: a person crossing from point A to point B in the midst of heart-stopping fear. It's a story all of us face. While we may not walk on a two-inch cable over a canyon, we all traverse the valley of fear to walk into our future.

Sharks

Hope is not available to us uncontested. It has age-old foes that are set on defeating us: anxiety and fear. While there are many well-known phobias, such as the fear of heights, dentists, spiders, and public speaking, a deeper kind of anxiety can affect us every day of our lives and stop us from stepping boldly into the full possibility of each moment. We can worry about disappointing others, dread what may happen if we're underachieving, be concerned about what others may think of us, or suffer with the uncertainty of what the future holds.

Me? I have a fear of sharks. Swimming in the ocean is a hard enough exercise, but the thought of a shark lurking beneath the waves is downright terrifying. When I swim at the beach, a dark shadow in the water is enough to trigger a momentary panic attack. The loss of control is what gets me—the thought that I am in their environment, vulnerable to attack by a hidden foe.

With that in mind, you can imagine my surprise when I read that mosquitoes kill more people in one day than sharks kill in one hundred years.[1] In fact, mosquitoes are the deadliest animal on earth, killing over half a million people every year by carrying diseases such as malaria and dengue fever. The reality is that I've never once worried about being fatally attacked by a mosquito. Spiders, yes. Sharks, absolutely. But a mosquito?

Why do I fear sharks more than mosquitos? It could be because I live in a country where the threat of contracting a fatal mosquito-borne disease is low, but I think it's for much more emotional and less technical reasons than that. Comedian Jerry Seinfeld once observed, "According to most studies, people's number one fear is public speaking. Number two is death. Death is number two. Does that sound right? This means to the average person, if you go to a funeral, you're better off in the casket than doing the eulogy."[2] Fear is not always logical.

If sharks don't get your pulse racing, let's take it up another level on the anxiety barometer. One spring afternoon, my dog started barking and going crazy outside. I went to see what all the commotion was about and saw a deadly eastern brown snake in my garden. They are one of the most venomous land snakes in the world, and they are highly aggressive. Google them—they are terrifying! And I was standing mere feet away, rescuing my dog from its reach. Thankfully, the snake slithered off into the forest.

The next day, I had to work in the same area of the garden. I was petrified. I had gloves and boots on, but I scanned every square inch of the garden. Suddenly, I heard a rustling sound. In that moment of danger, I thought I would do something useful, like run or shout for help. Instead, I felt a physical pain in my chest—and absolute terror. I couldn't move; I couldn't scream. I just froze.

I'm laughing as I write this because I'm a grown man, but I was physically overcome with terror at the thought of a snake. And, of course, it wasn't the snake coming back to seek its revenge on me—just a small pebble that had innocently rolled down an embankment. Imagine the fear Job had to overcome to truly live again. Worry would have been a constant companion as he tried to face his future. As he had more children and built a pathway through his pain, he would have had daily reminders of how things can go devastatingly wrong at any moment. Job would have felt anxious every time a messenger came to the door or every time there was a storm, worrying that history would repeat itself and something horrible would happen to his new children.

Job was confronted with a fear much broader than a phobia of a shark: he had to overcome his fear of the future. At some point, Job had to get up in the morning and begin to see that, despite his past, he still had a future. The loss never left. The pain was still real. However, Job had to look ahead, take all the trepidation and pain and grief in his heart, and decide that the future was full of possibility. He found a different ending to his story.

Before I had children of my own, I rarely struggled with daily anxiety. Yet, from the moment I drove home from the hospital with my firstborn son, who was swaddled in a white blanket with little mittens on his hands, I suddenly realized how delicate life is and how little control I have. I've wrestled with feelings of anxiety ever since. Every parent, at some point and in one way or another, has asked the question "What if something bad happens to my child?"

As a parent, I have the innate ability to visualize negative outcomes and how things could get worse for my children. I've wondered, "Why isn't my brain naturally wired to think of the best future? Why do I worry and fret and despair?" Intellectually, I know it comes from a deep, primal love for my kids. And I know it doesn't help me—or them—but I've often felt unable to shake a feeling of fear about something truly awful happening. I'm trying to retrain myself to have a more hopeful posture, but it's a work in progress.

Every person experiences fear and anxiety, whether a parent or not. The shark and the mosquito are archetypes of how fear and anxiety operate. The shark is visually menacing. The mosquito is tiny. Yet, in reality, it is the mosquito that is potentially a greater threat. The point is not that we should fear mosquitoes. It is that often fear is irrational, and if we let it dictate our future, we are following a false narrative.

Despite this truth, so often in life we are scared of sharks. We are fearful of scenarios and events that have large teeth and lurk in the shadows, and even the thought of those things possibly playing out in our lives brings terror. How much of our virtue is wasted worrying about the risk of being hurt, or the dread of being alone, or the fear of failure? How many years of our lives does anxiety steal from us? I have wasted too much time fearing "sharks." Worst-case outcomes that only exist in my imagination. Would you join me in no longer allowing these false fears to hold us back? Let's jump into the water of life!

I recently spoke to a friend; he had never experienced anxiety before, but one day he found himself curled up under his desk at work as an uncontrollable panic attack took over his mind and body. His day started like any other, but it ended with him sedated, taken to a hospital in an ambulance.

Anxiety is the emotional rehearsal of the worst-case scenario.

Anxiety is the emotional rehearsal of the worst-case scenario. I've personally found that anxiety is a form of artificial control. It can bring a comfort of sorts as we try to convince ourselves that our stress and anxiety over the future will somehow lessen the odds of something bad happening. But the reality is that no matter how much we worry about something, anxiety does not improve outcomes.

Nearly all the statistics on mental health provide a picture that seems as if we are using a broom to keep the tide of depression and anxiety out. So much human progress, so much technological wonder, so much innovation. Yet we are stressed like never before. For example, the Benson-Henry Institute estimates that 60–90 percent of visits to the doctor are stress related.[3]

It's not that hope completely removes all anxiety from our lives; that hasn't been the case for me or anyone I know. Hope is a learned skill. It is an intentional worldview, a deliberate choice we make to not allow stress and anxiety to dominate our emotions. And in a world that is drowning in the modern-day flood of depression, fear, and stress, we need to embrace something that goes deeper than breathing exercises, turning off social media, or cardio workouts. I mean, these are all positive things that I have benefited from, but they are no remedy for the assault on our mental health that we are trying to cope with.

A virtue like hope is something that permeates deep into the heart of the issue. We need to make a choice to see our future in color instead of black and white. We must choose to grow from our pain. We must be determined to find the *turn* where good comes out of our suffering. And we must see all the tragedies and sorrows of life from the vantage point of eternity. More to come on this soon.

Hope is the only virtue that can help us defeat fear and anxiety. It was Nelson Mandela who said, "The brave man is not he who does not feel afraid, but he who conquers that fear."[4] Fear has power only when we don't face it. Your deepest anxieties and fears can be overcome by the virtue of hope.

The overwhelming majority of things I have worried about have never happened. We can't spend our lives afraid of sharks. Fear wants to partner with our past to keep us in the place of pain. When my hope for the future is more prominent than my fear of the unknown, hope wins.

I've begun to train myself to ask, "What if something incredible happens today? What if today is the greatest day of my life? What if there is an unexpected surprise? Perhaps a wonderful opportunity or blessing lies ahead of me, one that will change my life for the better." Tell yourself that good things are ahead. Positive expectation is like the warm afternoon sun beaming through the window of your soul.

In the same way that adversity and hope have a symbiotic relationship, so do fear and courage. Courage is not the absence of fear and worry. Rather, courage exists only when we're faced with the challenge of overcoming a specific fear. Some of the greatest achievements were fueled by fear. Scientific breakthroughs. Agricultural ingenuity. Business revolutions.

Achievement often starts when someone follows a dream inside their heart and surmounts a fear of failure, embarrassment, or bankruptcy. The fear often makes them more creative, more resilient, and even more determined. The bestselling author J. K. Rowling once said that her fear of being a failure as a poor, single parent made her determined to prove herself. Difficult upbringings and early challenges are often a common denominator among great achievers. When did you last hear a bestselling author say they got picked up by the first publishing house they tried, or an entrepreneur claim that their first product was a breakthrough success? Easy paths don't seem to forge greatness. Smooth seas don't make good sailors. The adversity is what makes us.

Adversity teaches us things that only come to us when we have to deal with the problems of life, such as:

- being grateful for the simple things in life
- slowing down and recalibrating our perspective on success

- reexamining our beliefs and convictions—letting our root system grow deeper

Fear is combustible material; it can either burn down our future or it can fuel our forward movement. Fear can paralyze us or propel us. Use fear to thrust yourself forward. The same demanding project that stops someone from getting out of bed can cause another person to go to work an hour early to tackle it. Often, fears are a signpost to alert us that something incredible is on the other side.

Many of us suffer a slow-burn kind of anxiety that just simmers away, doing great damage over time. Yes, there will be sharp bursts of adversity that shock our lives with significant trauma, but don't ignore the long-term damage that can be caused by giving in to stress in your normal, everyday life.

Fear is combustible material; it can either burn down our future or it can fuel our forward movement.

The battle against fear occurs every day. I've chosen to stop being a passive victim of thoughts of fear by actively fighting them with thoughts of good. Dare to dream again. If you have another day, you have another opportunity at life.

Optimism

One of the most significant developments in psychology over the last fifty years is the realization that not all the answers can be found by diving into people's pasts, or by understanding their brokenness, fears, and phobias. Lasting change, healing, and progress occur only when people have a God-given vision of their future. This *learned* optimism is now a scientifically verifiable human trait.[5]

Hope is a risk. In its cleanest form, hope inflates the potential of feeling disappointment. It's not that hoping increases the odds of failure. But there is something to be said about our fear of getting our hopes up.

Our trepidation about embracing an optimistic mindset for the future can be crippling. We want to avoid the agony of *false* hope, in which we desire a positive outcome only to be disappointed. There is even a name for this behavior: defensive pessimism.[6] It is an intentional choice to imagine negative outcomes. If you have ever been disappointed or disillusioned, it may feel safer, or even strategic, to hedge your bets and imagine failure rather than dare to believe for a better future.

> **The very best thing we can do, when in pain, is actually to get our hopes up as high as we can!**

We may succumb to the temptation and allow our emotional state to accept fear and fatalism, but I struggle to see any benefit that pessimism brings into our lives. Hope is worth the risk. Getting one's hopes up is always worth it. When disappointment, hurt, or failure exist, that's when hope is at its best. So, the very best thing we can do when in pain is actually to get our hopes up as high as we can!

Better to hope big and fail than choose not to hope in the first place. Why? The virtue of hope changes us and, therefore, has the potential to change where our journey takes us. Hope makes the journey more joyful.

I don't think we are ever at risk of being *too* hopeful. It isn't as if, somehow, we have to ration our hope as a rare commodity. No, if there is a risk, it is that hope is scarce, and negativity is in abundance. Study after study shows us that being positive and optimistic improves our quality of life: it improves friendships, marriages, physical health, and life expectancy. Hope is not supposed to be used in small measures, but liberally.

It is better to live a life that is somehow too positive, too optimistic, and too full of anticipation for good things than to live in fear.

In our modern world, we are quickly given labels that end up defining not just *what* we have gone through but often *who* we are as people. If a tragedy becomes our identity, it alters the way we see ourselves and our future. Like a drop of royal blue ink in a glass of water, our entire life can get colored by negativity. Our self-talk, expectations of the future, and belief in others all get tainted with pessimism.

Pain can originate from trauma but grow into something else. I remember when I fell playing basketball and landed on my back. It hurt immediately, but the real challenge came months later when the pain worsened significantly. The doctor told me that a sudden trauma can shock the brain's pathways and cause the muscles all around the point of impact to seize up and go into protection mode. This protection mode, if not rehabilitated, can lead to stiffness and a lack of range of motion, which is exactly what had happened to me. Going into protection mode created even greater problems than the original injury.

The solution? My assumption was more rest. But in this situation, the advice was to start bringing movement back to the area that experienced the trauma. I remember the words of the doctor: "Exercise heals."

The right movements, done with the correct mechanics, can build strength and mobility. It's the same with our emotions. We all go through trauma—be it sickness, emotional breakdown, family conflict, unexpected world events. And it hurts. It brings pain. But it can cause areas of our soul to go into protection mode, and over time this can cause those areas of our heart to seize up. How many never love again? Never dream again? Never aspire again?

Don't allow one scene in the movie of your life to become the central plot. That's not to diminish the reality of the pain you have experienced, but the narrative of your life is about a greater purpose. Believe that what you are currently walking through is an unexpected twist in the story, but the glorious unfolding of the metaplot is yet to be revealed! I have spoken with a man who said he would never smile again after losing his brother. I have seen the hidden sting in the eyes of a father who lost his little girl. I have listened to a woman who was facing the betrayal of her husband's infidelity. If any of these—or an endless variety of other terrible sorrows—becomes your identity, then you will start to live out of that pain for the rest of your life. Remember: trauma can be devastating, but we don't have to let it define the core identity of who we are as people. Hope must remain central in our identity.

Pessimism is easy. We don't need to *try* to worry or construct scenarios of fear about the future, because our brains naturally do that for us! It's not more intellectual or advanced to subscribe to a pessimistic outlook on life. Psychologist Martin Seligman writes, "Helplessness in humans is ubiquitous and the source of endless suffering."[7] Instead of allowing our minds to be hardened by bitterness or a fatalistic attitude about the future, we need to find *healthy* pathways forward. How we respond to pain is crucial. Pain in life may be the pruning that leads to fruit.

Depression, anxiety, and a host of other ailments are significantly improved when people develop an optimistic approach to life. Our past cannot give us what we need for the future. Hope is vital. We can't live without something to look forward to.

Don't underestimate the health benefits of a positive outlook on life, nor the consequences of allowing stress to go unchecked.

If I can't change it, why worry about it?

If I can't change it, why regret it?

If I can't change it, why despair over it?

If I'm going to believe anything about the future, why not believe the very best?

In our world, fear has become the new normal. Our generation is seeing mega shifts in political power. National economies are collapsing under oceans of insurmountable debt. Pandemics, wars, and famines occur all around the globe. Natural disasters seem to be breaking all the records on a consistent basis. How often do we hear of the biggest earthquake, tsunami, or hurricane in history?

I would not be surprised if you had a specific anxiety weighing on your heart as you read this. This is the story for most of us. It's easy to become stressed and cynical. I know this feeling myself. Every day, when I read the news, I am reminded of the broken world in which we live. Another company going bankrupt, causing people to lose their jobs.

Another horrific school shooting. Barely a day goes by when we don't have to face some form of fear.

Jesus once posed this question: "Can all your worries add a single moment to your life?" (Matthew 6:27 NLT). It's a captivating question. Does all the worry and anxiety I live with help me in any way?

As an experiment, I wrote down the top five things I was stressing about when I was feeling overcome with worry. I asked myself, "Will this affect my life in one year? In five years? In fifty years?" Amazingly, I found the longer the timeline, the more likely I was to answer no. I discovered that the short-term, run-of-the-mill life issues were weighing me down. And that fear itself was more debilitating than the actual outcome I was fearing! Fear robs us of energy that could have been better used to fuel hope for the future.

Anxiety can prevent us from pursuing our dreams. Worry can stop us from believing in the best for the future. Uncertainty can hold us back from unexpected changes that open new doors. So tackle your fear. Wage war on it. Don't let fear win. If you have a fear of heights, stand on a bridge. When fear causes you to imagine the worst possible outcome, replace it in your mind with the best possible outcome. Fear can be turned into a positive when you realize that every fear is a door you have not yet opened. It's showing you a room of untapped possibility on the other side.

How many businesses never start due to fear of failure? How many public speeches were never made because of fear? How many hours of our lives have we wasted by dreading hypothetical outcomes?

Hope is the great antidote to a life of fear. Maybe you are constantly worried or suffering from sleepless nights of anxiety over what the future holds. It's important not to allow a fear of "sharks" to keep you from the ocean of your future.

Nik Wallenda showed the world that there is always something positive on the other side of fear. The journey of tomorrow only begins when we let go of the fears of yesterday. If hope can open new doors to our future, fear wants to slam the doors closed. Embrace the risk of stepping into an unknown future, even if you're afraid. For almost every great achievement, every significant season of growth, and every beautiful thing that exists in your future, you must walk through anxiety and fear.

What would you do if you had no fear?

I've heard it said that we can live about forty days without food, about three days without water, and about seven minutes without oxygen—but not a second without hope. Therefore, don't lose the battle to fear or worry in your mind. Fight for optimism. At our core, the native human language is hope, not fear. We are wired to lean toward the light. Your brightest possibilities are just one step past your darkest fears.

The most terrible poverty is loneliness, and the feeling of being unloved.

—Mother Teresa

CHAPTER 8

200 Hands

Hope flows through friendship

PICTURE THE SCENE. It's June 2018, northern Thailand. Twelve boys and their soccer coach are trapped deep underground in the Tham Luang Nang Non cave. Their situation is dire.

When you think of this cave, please don't imagine a little cavity in the side of a mountain. No. This cave is more like a long, maze-like tunnel. A labyrinth of dark underground chambers and channels.

These twelve boys and their coach are trapped more than a mile and a half from the opening. They are sitting on an elevated rock shelf with only torches in the pitch darkness, starving and desperate.

Culturally, it is a rite of passage for the boys to crawl through these tunnels during the dry season, overcoming their fear. After training, they entered the cave, only to become trapped by sudden rain that flooded their only way out.

When the children do not return home, parents and another soccer coach race to the cave opening, only to find bicycles and personal belongings strewn on the ground, and dark, muddy water seeping out from the tunnel. It's a gut-wrenching scene. Something has gone terribly wrong.

For almost two weeks, the boys sit trapped with no contact from the outside world. On the surface, a now-famous worldwide effort gets underway. Ten thousand people participate in a massive international effort to rescue the boys.

But in the cave, the boys are isolated and alone. Two weeks is no small amount of time to sit in the proverbial belly of a whale! On the surface, parents are desperate. They weep. They pray. They hold vigils and comfort each other, fearing the worst.

With dangerous monsoon rains threatening to completely flood the cave and oxygen running out, the rescue teams race to save the boys and their coach from the horrible fate of either drowning or suffocating.

The rescue operation is fascinating on many levels. It is immensely complex and requires detailed planning and logistics. Thai Navy SEALs and other open-water divers from around the world are unsuccessful in their initial rescue attempts. Some sections of the cave are too narrow to wear a scuba tank. The murky water offers almost no visibility. One experienced rescuer tragically drowns.

Even highly trained military units do not have the specialized experience to navigate the flooded tunnels. So, the rescue operation turns to a handful of private cave divers to lead the retrieval of the children. These cave divers, most of whom are amateur enthusiasts with hand-modified equipment, are the only ones with the special expertise to undertake the rescue. They are largely weekend hobbyists, but they have spent years practicing in the niche area of extreme cave diving. They are unlikely candidates.

With extensive planning, and the international media looking on, the divers attempt to retrieve the children one by one from the cave. The children are sedated, oxygen masks are fixed to their faces, and they are literally dragged out by the divers over muddy rocks and through narrow, flooded crevices.

The cave divers are heroic, but bringing the children through the water is not the end of the rescue. The children must be transported from an underground section of the cave, called chamber three, to the surface.

What the rescuers do next is ingenious and serves as a profound lesson for us all: approximately two hundred people form a human chain along a pulley system. As each child is brought up out of the water, they are lifted and slid and passed hand by hand to the surface.

On July 10, 2018, after 18 days, the last child is rescued. It is a miracle. The children and their coach are still alive.

I'm amazed by the skill and courage of the divers, but I'm captivated by this simple, rudimentary phase of the rescue of children being passed along a human conveyor belt of outstretched hands.

It took two hundred people to bring each child up from chamber three to freedom.

Here's the question that gripped my imagination: "Which of the two hundred sets of hands saved the child?"

The first set? The last set?

Perhaps we could make the case that *all* sets of hands equally saved the children!

These children experienced hope, and yet that hope was provided to them by a *community* of people.

Hope and community go hand in hand. We need others.

There was a small group of six leading divers. There was also a hands-on community of two hundred others. Another ten thousand people were involved in the extended rescue teams, too. These numbers don't form precise categories, but there is something in the various levels of community that we need in our lives. We *need* a handful of close friends. We *need* a rich sense of community with anywhere from fifty to two hundred people who we are in some form of contact with. Let's not forget that we *need* to find meaning in the broader network and city we are a part of (represented by the ten thousand people involved in the cave rescue).

> **Pain is amplified in the cold rain of loneliness, but it is divided in the warmth of community.**

I've been thinking a lot about the following question: "Is there a link between friendship and hope?" I've often seen hope as more of an internal, private experience—something that happens in me as an individual. But I'm starting to see that hope is a communal experience. For me to truly experience the tide-turning power of hope, I *need* others.

Hope needs human skin.

This is important to recognize, as we are living in an era where our worldview is hyper individualized. We have soaring levels of loneliness and isolation. Research by the Barna Group found that one out of every three adults said they felt lonely, and that feelings of loneliness have doubled in the past twenty-five years.[1]

In one study, 22 percent of Millennials said they had no friends.[2] Zero. Alone on an island. It's stunning to think almost a quarter of this generation feels like they don't have a single person in the world to turn to in times of need. Gen Z is even worse. According to a survey done by Cigna, nearly 79 percent of Gen Z respondents reported feeling lonely.[3]

We all face tribulations, but it is the combination of facing these challenges while at the *same time* feeling loneliness that we need to address. I'm not sure where I first heard it, but I tell my kids all the time, "A problem shared is a problem halved."

Yet, many of us feel like we don't have friends, or a community, to share our problems with. Pain is amplified in the cold rain of loneliness, but it is divided in the warmth of community.

Author Jennie Allen writes, "We spend hours alone in our crowded, noisy, screen-lit worlds, we invest only sporadic time with acquaintances, and then we expect close friends to somehow appear in our busy lives."[4] She's onto something! I know what it is to feel loneliness and isolation. I may be scrolling on my phone, or have people all around me, but I still feel disconnected from everyone. Although it is irrational, sometimes I have feelings rise within me when I'm in a large crowd of people, or a house full of family and friends, feelings like, *Does anybody really know what I am feeling? And, more importantly, does anyone truly care?*

Hopelessness and loneliness are co-conspirators to our undoing.

This brings me to Job's three friends. In the historical understanding of the life of Job, these guys are viewed as villains. They are the well-intentioned friends who offer up bad advice, heaping trauma on Job's life.

However, I've come to see these three friends through a different lens.

Job's three friends

Reading from Job 2:11–13:

> When three of Job's friends heard of the tragedy he had suffered, they got together and traveled from their homes to comfort and console him. Their names were Eliphaz the Temanite, Bildad the Shuhite, and Zophar the Naamathite. When they

saw Job from a distance, they scarcely recognized him. Wailing loudly, they tore their robes and threw dust into the air over their heads to show their grief. Then they sat on the ground with him for seven days and nights. No one said a word to Job, for they saw that his suffering was too great for words.

Job has just lost everything and is paralyzed with grief. He feels completely alone. In fact, Job goes on to say that in his suffering, most of his friends have abandoned him: "My family is gone, and my close friends have forgotten me" (Job 19:14). Think about it. Absolute rock bottom, and alone. What hurt more—the physical discomfort of sitting on the ground and the boils on his skin, or the sting of being isolated?

Sometimes, the people you thought would be there for you are nowhere to be seen. This can hurt more than the impact that caused the pain in the first place!

Add to that, Job's season of being alone seems to last for a long time. He speaks of long nights of misery and months of being alone (see Job 7:3).

It's possible that months go by before the time the three friends arrive. I want you to picture the scene. Job has been through a terrifying season of grief. He has lost his kids, his wealth, and his health. He is completely alone, sitting in the dirt of the earth, heaping ashes over his face. On the horizon, through the dried tears on his dusty face, Job sees the distant outline of three men. As they draw closer, the friends struggle to recognize Job, as he is physically disfigured because of his grief.

Think of the dramatic contrast!

The Job they knew was a prominent and immensely wealthy man. If they ever saw Job at his peak, they would be familiar with seeing him in fine clothes, confident, and eating and drinking with his family. They can't believe it is him! Yet, at some point, Job recognizes them. They are not random travelers. They are familiar faces. They are friends. Can you imagine the emotion Job felt at that very moment? Job has lost so much. But oh, the richness of life that is found in his friendship with these three men! Something of value remains in his life. Hope walks into his life in the form of three friends.

It is likely that these friends had shared memories with Job and his family in his home when he was flourishing. But they also came to sit with him on the ground. That's true friendship. I've often found that people are willing to sit with me during seasons of my life when success and favor abound, but when I've found myself broken on the ground, it takes a true friend who will sit with me then!

It reminds me of my favorite quote on friendship: "A friend is one who walks in when the rest of the world walks out."[5] This quote has been attributed to many since the early 1900s, but it is as relevant now as it was then. Maybe in his success Job had three hundred friends, or three thousand, but only *three* walk into his pain.

The dramatic moment Job's three friends walk into his grief is perhaps the most special moment in this entire story. These three individuals have come together and made an intentional plan to travel to Job and provide comfort. They leave their homes. They leave their families. They are not going on a vacation. They are not going to the beach. They are going to *be* friends.

To reference our earlier story of the Thai cave, these three friends are like the divers. They are entering the dark waters, and they are swimming toward Job. When they find him, their response is one of deep empathy. The three friends sit with Job in silence on the ground. They weep with him. They throw dust toward heaven and let it fall on their faces. They show up, not just physically but emotionally.

Sometimes, things are too raw to talk about. Or it feels as if there is no way you can put into words how you feel and what you are going through. Being physically present matters. If I take a Polaroid in my mind and capture the moment of the men sitting together on the ground in silence, it is a tragic and yet beautiful picture of community.

Everyone else seemingly forsakes Job, but not these friends. Sometimes, you don't need three hundred. You don't need a crowd. You don't need a following. You need three friends to walk in when the whole world walks out.

The great act of friendship? Job's suffering becomes their suffering, and shared suffering is the opening of the window to hope.

Pain needs to be diffused through our friendships to come out the other side as hope.

Hope ambassadors

I've also experienced another interesting thing. Often, when I look back at my life and see a turn toward the positive, an open door, a provision, or even some kind of divine intervention, it has come at the hands of a person.

I'm not sure the words *hope* and *alone* are compatible. We were created for community. We are relational beings.

When I look for the fingerprints of the divine in my life, I often look for something that appears to be remarkable or potentially even mystical—that clearly seems like an answer from heaven.

Have you ever asked God for a sign? I know I have. Or do you long for an emotional feeling, or a dramatic reversal of challenging circumstances that you can clearly label? Only God can do that. And if and when those things happen in your life, how wonderful! But to be transparent with you, I have discovered that when God wants to bring hope into my life, it's not necessarily through heavenly experiences where the sky parts or my problems are magically erased. In reflecting on my life, I can report that the most common way I've seen God show up in my life has been through the blessing of people.

It's fascinating that this also seems to be the lesson throughout the arc of the biblical narrative. There is a clear pattern. When people were in pain, God sent a person. Examples include the fierce loyalty of Jonathan as a friend to David (1 Samuel 18). Aaron being the trusted spokesperson for Moses (due to his nerves and speech problems). Ruth refusing to abandon Naomi (Ruth 1:16–17). Epaphroditus visiting the apostle Paul, who was in chains and in the darkness of a prison cell (Philippians 2:25). And, ultimately, Jesus being sent as the Savior for all humanity (John 15:13).

Hope feels warm. Amber. Relational. Human.

Think about this: God could use literally anything to be His special dispenser of hope. He could simply orchestrate circumstances to deliver hope; He could just unilaterally change things in our lives without involving anyone. But in His array of tools, the great Doctor has one that is His tool of choice. The tool that God uses to bring hope is *people*.

Over and over again in Scripture, God used a person to be the conduit for meeting the needs of others. It doesn't mean the people are divine, or even particularly remarkable or special. No—God used everyday people to bring remarkable hope. The same thing happens in our lives. God still uses everyday people to step into our lives as *hope ambassadors*. Parents. Old school friends. The lady doing your hair. The barista serving your coffee. The stranger next to you on the bus. These instances can be more than a serendipitous crossing of paths. At crucial moments in your life, look for hope ambassadors.

I was deeply moved by the memoir of Holocaust survivor Eddie Jaku. In his bestselling memoir, *The Happiest Man on Earth*, which was published when he was one hundred years old, he writes about the qualities that enabled him not just to survive the Auschwitz concentration camp during World War II but to then rebuild his life and live with joy and meaning. The atrocities he had to live through were shocking and gut-wrenching. How could someone who lost so much, and endured such deep pain, go on to be described by his own family as "the happiest man on earth"?

Eddie helps us to understand what helped him the most:

> This is the most important thing I have ever learned: the greatest thing you will ever do is be loved by another person.
>
> I cannot emphasize this enough, especially to young people. Without friendship, a human being is lost. A friend is someone who reminds you to feel alive. . . . One good friend can be your entire world.
>
> This, more than the food we shared or the warm clothes or the medicine, was the most important thing. The best balm for the soul is friendship. And with that friendship, we could do the impossible.[6]

Job had three friends. But in the most atrocious of human conditions that Eddie experienced, he found even a single friend was a total game changer. He found hope not just in the thought that one day he might be free, or in positive thinking, or in imagining a miraculous escape. Rather, hope came to him in the form of a solitary friend—and that was enough.

Hope is not an emotion or a feeling. It seems to be much more tangible than that. It comes to us through real people, friendships, and community. It is less about dramatic, heavenly moments of the skies parting and a lightning strike of provision, and more about earthly moments of grounded relational warmth that bring about something of an infusion of grace to make it through our challenges.

Hope is not an emotion or a feeling. It seems to be much more tangible than that. It comes to us through real people, friendships, and community.

For some reason, we often conceptualize hope as a sort of ethereal, intangible experience. A deep experience of the soul. Almost hidden from human sight and intervention. We tend not to see it as practical. In fact, it may feel like talking about friendship and community is a tangent to a conversation about pain and hope. But not for me. In my mind, it is central. When we start to see hope not as a mystical force but as a relational quality, this grounds it in the reality of our human experience. We need people, and we need to be there for people.

Hope is less an emotional force and more a relational practice. Yes, it is a spark in the human heart. It is possible that it can arise in solitary confinement, but we are relational beings who need others. True friendship is one of the greatest dispensers of hope that exists.

Remember the Grant and Glueck studies by Harvard we talked about earlier? They involved 724 men who were studied and tracked by Harvard for more than seventy-five years, and were examined to determine what makes for a happy life. Robert Waldinger was the fourth director of this study and an active participant since 1938. He shared the top finding in his Ted Talk:

> The clearest message that we get from this 75-year study is this: Good relationships keep us happier and healthier. Period. . . . Our study has shown that the people who fared the best were the people who leaned in to relationships, with family, with friends, with community. . . . The good life is built with good relationships.[7]

The study also revealed that loneliness and isolation are toxic to our lives and cause a decline in our brain activity.

What enabled some men to respond better to the trials and challenges that life brought their way was having good quality relationships. This furthers my thesis that hope flows through friendships. When the participants went through trauma, such as a job loss, the death of a spouse, a disease, or any number of major life catastrophes, the single leading predictor of their ability to practice adaptive coping was the quality of their relationships—especially close relationships. If we want an ecosystem in our lives that yields the fruit of hope for us and makes optimism available to us, we need to develop friendships and community at a deeper level.

If you are at a point in your life where it feels like it is too late for that, start with those closest to you. The nurse in your hospital room. The family member whom you can call. Reach out to whoever has relational proximity to you right now.

The idea of hope ambassadors flows two ways. The old saying is true—to make a friend, be a friend. Become a hope ambassador for someone in need. People carry more pain than we realize. It's hard to detect, because there is often no physical identifier that somebody is feeling lonely, woeful, traumatized, or crippled with fear. You can be standing right next to someone who is talking and laughing, yet have no idea that they are in the midst of an inescapable sense of dread or despair. Yes, sometimes you get glimpses of what someone is feeling within. The brief welling of tears in a friend's eyes as they talk about their childhood. The little phrases that suggest there is a lot more left unsaid. Pain camouflages. Yet every single person has a unique story of adversity and trials. Being aware of this makes us open and empathetic to the people in our world. It pushes us to look beneath the surface and seek a connection to the heart.

When you remember a story of someone who just received a cancer diagnosis, or went through a major life transition, or is struggling with loneliness—it could be any number of life-changing things—instead of just *hearing* about it and being moved emotionally, why not initiate contact and communicate with that person? I've found the pattern of doing this once a week for six months helpful. I call this "going on the journey" with someone. It's more than just a one-off message. It is consistently checking in over a period of time.

Community and friendship are not just something we receive. There is healing in the giving of friendship. We never know the exact role our hands play in the chain that helps rescue another. Sometimes it seems like we only did something small to make a difference, but, like the human chain of two hundred rescuers in the Thai cave, you passed someone forward. You helped an individual take the next step.

Serve others, knowing that your role in the chain of human interaction is crucial in their destiny. You may be one of two hundred in that person's story—but your hands helped that person's transformation as much as anyone else's.

There's no such thing as making a small difference in someone's life. The person you greet. The young person you mentor. The friend you encourage. You are part of a human chain on an assignment from God to help move others toward freedom in life.

The friends speak

Back to Job's friends. They travel to sit with him for seven days. What a beautiful picture! After seven days, they decide to process out loud the trauma and pain that Job has experienced. They try to understand *why* Job has gone through something so shocking. They attempt to make rational sense of it all. And so it is, after seven days of great friendship, they open their mouths and give terrible advice. In fact, the advice is so bad that these three friends are now remembered most for their poorly worded responses to Job. They blame Job. They mischaracterize God. They throw around wild theories as to why his bad luck happened.

There is no glossing over it. Their story is notorious for a reason. They would have been better off staying silent. The story of Job is filled with chapters of the three friends expressing a flawed perspective: that when people go through suffering, it is because they did something wrong. It gets so bad that Job responds, "How long will you torture me? How long will you try to crush me with your words?" (Job 19:2). Yes—I guess we can conclude their prose is hurtful, not helpful!

Unfortunately, that has become the legacy, or almost the legend, of these three friends. The story is now told of how there were three bad friends that came and gave bad advice. But I'm seeing something much more nuanced here that challenges this widely believed narrative.

Yes, history shows that Job's friends offered bad advice, and yet this does not mean that the net effect of these friends was negative or terrible. In fact, a case could be made that despite their bad advice, the very fact that Job had such close friends and was able to process his trauma with them overrides the poor advice that was given.

Was the quality of their friendship measured by how sage their advice was? Or was it seen in them leaving their homes and their families and traveling to walk right into Job's pain? Think about it—this was no vacation! They didn't just send a letter of encouragement. They didn't keep their walls up. They wailed in grief, tore their robes, and threw dust over their faces. That's friendship. A stunning act of relational warmth and community.

This act of profound friendship is often overlooked. We get so caught up in the conversation that follows as the three friends try to process and understand why such terrible suffering crushed Job's life. Yes, they got their advice wrong. Their theories and ideas of why Job is experiencing this trauma just add to his pain. But I think we give these guys too hard a time. We forget the first seven days. At least they had the emotional intelligence in that moment not to speak. How many of us, when we have gone through loss or pain, have longed for just a single friend to walk into our lives and sit with us and just be present? Job had three.

I guess we will never know how Job would have handled this catastrophe if his friends had never shown up and sat with him during his loss. What we do know is that Job shared his suffering in community. Without that, Job would have had to endure a further wound: loneliness. Sure, the friends didn't get all their words right, but they showed up when it mattered most. It leads me to say this: community is often the conduit of hope.

Village of hope

I've often been on the receiving end of people bringing hope into my world. Sometimes, it is close to home. The very week of writing this I was languishing over a recent career setback. My wife, Cindi, saw the pain on my face. She sat with me and reminded me that I have a bright future, and I haven't yet seen how things will unfold. They were simple words of encouragement, but they brought hope into my heart. As a father, my children also bring me hope. A simple hug, a handwritten letter that says, "You're the best dad in the world." It doesn't take much to feel the burdens lift a little.

We need community. Sometimes, the lack of community is not due to isolation but rather insulation. When we go through pain, we often put walls up emotionally and retreat. To experience hope, we must push through that. Take the risk of being vulnerable and proactively invite people into your dust-and-ashes moments. Send a text: "I could really use a friend right now." Make a call: "Could we grab a coffee this week?" Or even physically get in the car and drive to a friend or family member and ask for help.

If you don't seem to have three friends walking into your pain, take the step to initiate the human exchange. Remember, one good friend can be your entire world.

Open your heart to hope. Open your heart to people. We must be vulnerable, intentional, and humble.

Here are some next steps to proactively build a village of hope:

- Strengthen family relationships (intentionally draw closer to those nearest you).
- Build an inner circle (remember the six divers and Job's three friends).
- Invest in a village (an extended community of church, sports teams, volunteer organizations, and interpersonal relationships).

Mother Teresa was once asked, "What's the biggest problem in the world today?" Her response is still relevant: "The biggest problem in the world today is that we draw the circle of our family too small. We need to draw it larger each day."[8] Let's draw the family larger. Let's be a friend to those in need. Let's be vulnerable and invite friends into our pain. Let's see hope as a human expression and not just a vague sentiment or force.

Hope is more than a feeling. Hope is a human exchange. It's an interpersonal flow from one person to another. Hope is found in belonging, in intimacy.

Hope flows through friendship.

Do one thing every day that scares you.

—Mary Schmich[1]

Watchmaker

Adversity + Hope = Resilience

I LOVE MECHANICAL WATCHES. In our modern digital era, there is something grounding about wearing a device that does not require electricity or a battery to operate.

On the surface, mechanical watches are artistic and beautiful, but hidden under their faces is masterful engineering that's been refined over centuries. In fact, a mechanical watch is similar to a car engine, but with components on a micro scale. Watches are made up of hundreds of tiny interconnected parts—such as rotors, springs, and gears—that can keep remarkably precise time.

Yet, no matter how ornate or decorative a watch is, if it cannot keep accurate time, it fails in its purpose.

It is here, in the history of mechanical watchmaking, that we can trace the etymology of the word *resilience*. Up until modern times, resilience was a technical term used to describe a material's ability to tolerate extreme pressure and return to its original form. Today, the word resilience is more commonly associated with behavioral science and refers to a person's ability to bounce back after trauma.

When we look back to the old-world use of the word, it deepens our understanding of this amazing human quality. In the nineteenth century, the word *resilient* was a technical term that watchmakers used to describe a watch's ability to absorb shock.[2] In fact, even to this day, the most advanced watch engineers in the world are still developing new innovations to make their internal hairsprings more resilient to vibrations.[3] The more resilient the internal components, the more reliable the watch.

During its lifetime, a watch will be subjected to different stressors. It could be bumped against a tree during a hike through a dense forest, pounded by waves during a dive into the ocean, or jolted as its wearer swings a hammer in construction. The possibilities of damage, once a watch leaves the protection of a glass cabinet, are as varied as the human experience. Where the wearer goes, the watch goes. Any jarring shock to the watch sends vibrations through its internal components. A watch that lacks resilience will be thrown off by the bumps and knocks that life brings. It will lose time. Its perfect internal symmetry and mechanics will be thrown out of rhythm. But a watch with highly resilient internal materials will be able to absorb the impacts of life and keep accurate time.

In the nineteenth century, the word resilient was a technical term that watchmakers used to describe a watch's ability to absorb shock.

This is not just about horology, but also humanity. Our ability to absorb circumstances and events in life that shock us is a crucial skill to learn. If our happiness is reliant on our lives being perfect, we will lack the ability to stand up to the inevitable rigors of disappointments, failures, and loss.

People can also lose time. Unexpected blows can reverberate through our entire being and throw off our internal rhythm. That's where developing resilience comes in. It gives us grit. Resilience is not a gift we are born with. It is more like a muscle we can develop over time as we wrestle with the strain of real-life problems.

Have you ever felt like giving up? I know I have.

I remember a season when my life felt like it was folding in on me. I had started a new business. There was financial pressure from the up-front investment. I had a newborn baby at home, and I was trying to be a good dad. I wanted to be a better husband and be home more. I felt like I had a lot of people I was responsible for. Amid that, I was trying to navigate my own journey as an individual. I had become so busy that I didn't have time for hobbies, or even friends. Feelings of loneliness had started to develop. It wasn't any one single crisis, but I had pressure and complexity in pretty much every main area of my life.

If it were just *one* of these challenges, I would have felt confident about overcoming it. But they formed a formidable alliance, and together they attacked my life at once. As the problems started to layer up, I felt myself reaching a breaking point.

Perhaps that feeling of challenges stacking up is something you can relate to. It's where life starts to feel overwhelming. When it all hits at the same time, it can bring about such force that even our physical bodies are affected. Lots of little pressures and pain points can add up and place an intense stretch on our emotions.

I had to ask myself, "How should I respond to this season of life?" Sometimes, we don't have the perfect quote in the moment. Often, we struggle to understand what the best next steps are. But in seasons when our life gets knocked, sometimes one of the greatest plays we have available is to absorb the impact and bounce back. Victory may be simply getting out of bed in the morning. Walking the dog. Showing up for work. Smiling at your spouse. We don't have to be absolutely soaring every moment of every year and dominating in every area of life. Sometimes, surviving is underrated.

For me, in that season, I made a decision. I didn't know how to untangle the thread, or the right moves to make. But I decided to absorb the pressure, stand, and, in time, recalibrate my life. That recalibration took over a year. I sold the business, changed my work schedule, and even moved to a new neighborhood that was more family friendly. What about you? Resilience is what we get when we act with hopeful intent in the middle of adversity. Is it possible that the bravest, most remarkable thing you could do is simply to survive the season you are in? To absorb it? To resolve within yourself that a brighter day is arriving tomorrow and your life will bounce back?

Resilience is hope in action.

Sometimes, by default, we perceive hope as a virtue and not as a set of concrete actions. Hope becomes something intangible and is grouped with wishful thinking or good intentions. But what if hope—real hope—had movement and action?

Resilience is hope in action. It is the ability to get back up when life knocks us down: a romance between adversity and hope. These two themes walk hand in hand through the journey of life.

There is something broken about our cultural narrative. We understand the good life. We pursue it. Success.

Opportunities. Influence. Recognition. Health. Happiness. We are good with the positive. But that leaves little room in our worldview for pain. We struggle to understand it. As a result, we spend a good portion of our lives trying to avoid challenges.

Ironically, when we talk about the moments that have fashioned and impacted our lives the most, we often talk about challenges, battles, and adversity. These are things that, at the time, seemed like setbacks—but now, when we talk about them, we see how they made us stronger. That's what resilience is.

In her book *Supernormal*, Meg Jay looks at the link between childhood adversity and resilience. She cites a 1955 study done on Kauai, Hawaii's "Garden Island," in which 698 infants were studied over a period of decades. Many had been born into families that faced immense adversity: chronic poverty, unemployment, alcoholism, mental illness, and lack of education. In other words, these babies were chosen as research subjects specifically because the odds were stacked against them from the moment they were born.

The researchers' initial hypothesis was as you would expect: the children who experienced the most hardship while growing up would also experience the most problems as adults. This is exactly what I would have presumed.

But the results were groundbreaking, and they turned some of the early predictions on their head. Surprisingly, about one third of the children considered high-risk went on to thrive. They often overcame substance abuse, earned better educations, and developed caring relationships. Jay writes, "What was intended to be an inquiry about the devastating impact of early adversity became a seminal work about the possibility of transcending it."[4]

The researchers had anticipated that these children would struggle and that addiction, poverty, and dysfunction would be their norm as they grew into adults. No wonder they were shocked when the opposite occurred.

As a father myself, I found these results very intriguing. No one is suggesting that we should intentionally make life hard for children, or that childhood poverty is a good thing. But this research does show us that disadvantages can help create resilience that is both surprising and powerful.

Though the children faced great difficulties, they also learned perseverance, strength, and an enhanced survival instinct that helped them find solutions in their lives.

My instinct is to want to step in and solve my kids' problems. Even little problems. I remember when I was teaching my firstborn son to play basketball. I would put him on my shoulders and lift him right up to the hoop, where he could drop the ball in. However, I had to begin to walk back my assistance to help my son develop his own strength and skills. I went from holding him at waist height, to him standing on the ground and shooting underarm, to eventually the day that he shot the basketball normally and got it in. If I had always put my son on my shoulders to shoot a basketball, he would never have developed his own abilities. That's what practicing resilience does. It is never static. It develops new parts of who we are as people.

Adversity never feels like a positive thing. No one in the midst of a trauma wakes up in the morning and says, "This feels fantastic!" But we can train ourselves to value the end result of adversity by understanding how it helps us to grow stronger.

Eucalyptus

Eucalyptus trees carpet my native country of Australia. I remember walking through a forest that had recently been scorched by a fire. The ground was still covered with black ash, and a strong smell of smoke hung in the air, but bright green shoots had already begun to sprout. After a few months, the charred landscape had given birth to countless new eucalyptus trees.

I was astonished to see how this resilient species of tree had used the fire as an opportunity to multiply!

After a fire sweeps through an area, eucalyptus trees have an advantage over other plants. Their seed capsules open when burned, and the seedlings thrive in freshly burned, ash-rich soil. In fact, certain species actually require the tough coating around the seed to be melted by fire in order to germinate. It's not just a story of surviving a fire—it's better than that. It's that the fire is *necessary* in order for the potential to be birthed. There's a certain drama to it.

This remarkable feature of eucalyptus trees has helped them dominate landscapes.[5] Think about it for a moment. *The same fire that brings devastation is also the key that unlocks new life.*

If you are experiencing a wildfire in your own life, who knows what seeds can shoot up through the soil when it's over?

Greenlight

The full spectrum of human experience includes both beauty and pain. Often, they are in a dance together and we see

143

the value of our struggles only when looking back. Academy Award–winning actor Matthew McConaughey writes, "The problems we face today eventually turn into blessings in the rearview mirror of life. In time, yesterday's red light leads us to a greenlight."[6] In fact, I find it fascinating that almost every autobiography I have read features its author's disadvantaged start to life, or their triumph over a season of immense crisis and tragedy that came to define their legacy.

Have you ever wondered why one of the constant themes in the lives of high achievers is how an early failure laid the foundation for a remarkable future? Business moguls whose products didn't sell. Sporting icons cut from their high school teams. Scientists whose experiments failed dozens of times. Innovators whose prototypes took hundreds of trials. Careers started by packing shelves in midnight shifts at supermarkets. Me? I worked in a chicken factory!

Obstacles can create opportunities. Adversity can become an advantage.

It's not rare to hear these kinds of stories. In almost all of these cases, the struggle builds strength. The hardest weight to carry can forge resilience for the future. Fire destroys, but pottery is finished because of the furnace's heat. A bow that is pulled back intensely can fire the arrow that travels farthest. Obstacles can create opportunities. Adversity can become an advantage.

Practically speaking, resilience means we carry a flexibility in our lives that we can draw on when things don't work out the way we want. It means that when one area of our life is experiencing adversity, we keep a broad enough perspective to see the good in the other aspects of our life. If Option A doesn't work out, resilience asks what Option B is. Resilience accepts the pressures and shocks of life, flexes under their weight without breaking, and over time helps us to spring back. It means that we push ourselves to persevere and not to give up, even if we are standing in the ashes of failure.

Resilience is underrated. The ability to simply stand. Anyone can sustain hope on sunny days. Anyone can sing, pray, praise, and trust when the seas are smooth. But I have yet to hear a person's story who has only ever experienced smooth seas. At some point in our lives, the swell starts to rise. The wind picks up. Resilience is the ability to stand. And hope that cannot stand the trauma of real life, no matter how articulate or beautiful, is not true hope. But a gritty, less professional hope that is robust in the face of suffering—that is something very special. Resilience must be constructed in our soul and our worldview brick by brick. It must be a series of choices that we make regarding how we see the story of God woven with the story of our humanity.

Resilience means I'm still standing. I may be windbeaten. Debris may be everywhere. The furniture on the deck may have been swept away. Leaves and trees may have fallen. But when the sun finally emerges, I'm still standing. I'm still here.

The hope that Job expressed was a resilient one. This resilience enabled him to flex under the pressure and not break. And, given time, it enabled him to bounce back and rebuild his life.

When faced with unimaginable heartbreak, Job said, "When he tests me, I will come out as pure as gold" (Job

23:10). Job saw the great tests of life as a refining process. When gold is mined from the earth, the ore goes through a series of treatments that remove impurities. Eventually, all the surrounding dirt and unwanted minerals are removed, and all that is left is pure gold. Job could have seen the trauma he faced as hopeless devastation. But because he had a resilient outlook, he saw the fiery trials as a refining process that would make him into the man he was born to be. Job's example is whispering a life lesson to us: resilience sees gold where others see dirt.

Building resilience should be approached in the same way we build physical health. We don't think of physical health as the result of a single event or the one day we chose to exercise. Rather, physical health is developed through daily movement. Doctors are constantly telling us to walk more, stand instead of sit, and increase our heart rate every day. Our inner world is very similar, and we can look for ways to develop resilience right now. Resilience is functional hope.

Adversity + Stress = Anxiety

Adversity + Hope = Resilience

If necessity is the mother of invention, then adversity surely is the mother of resilience.

Where to look? Start with wherever you are feeling stress. Whether it's a work project, a family relationship, or a financial strain, don't allow it to break you. The same pressure that is causing you to bend will ultimately propel you back as you rebound in life. Don't give up. Bounce back. Embrace the positive.

You are stronger than you could possibly imagine.

Watches keep time when their hidden internal materials have resilient properties. They can absorb shock, neglect, and trauma and still maintain their rhythm. Humans are no different. Bumps and knocks will come, but what happens *within* us is more important than what happens *to* us. We keep flourishing and growing when the hidden inner workings of our soul use the strain of life to build resilience.

If you know how, and when, to deal with life's challenges—how to get relative with the inevitable—you can enjoy a state of success I call "catching greenlights."

—Matthew McConaughey[1]

Submarine

Have faith in God

DECEMBER 1927: the USS *S-4* submarine was conducting routine trials off Cape Cod. Typically, submarines use periscopes to survey the water's surface before they ascend. But, on this fateful day, something went horribly wrong. The *S-4* surfaced in the path of the hulking Coast Guard destroyer *Paulding*.

The alarm sounded on the deck of the *Paulding*, but a collision could not be avoided. The impact was devastating.

The *S-4*'s hull was ripped open and the sub started to sink. The forty-person crew heard the sound of water flooding their submarine. The smell of salty seawater filled the air. The scene was chaos. The crew made a panicked set of decisions under extreme pressure. Chlorine gas swept the control room, and an electrical fire broke out. With just moments to react, thirty-four of the crew decided to lock themselves in one room. As their throats burned from gas inhalation, they closed the valves and sealed the door from the inside.

As water began to penetrate the seals, they improvised with desperate measures, using planks of timber to reinforce the door. But the freezing water kept bursting through the seals. The small chamber was claustrophobic, with barely any room to stand—every breath created a toxic surplus of carbon dioxide.

All thirty-four died.

Remarkably, six men in another room remained alive, sealed in the watertight torpedo chamber. They sat in darkness, haunted by the sounds of their fellow crew members dying in the next chamber. At 102 feet below the surface, they waited. Hours. And then days. The Navy made repeated dives and frantic attempts to save them. The survivors' supply of oxygen declined rapidly.

As the six men huddled together in that dark torpedo chamber, they tapped messages on the steel hull to the rescuers. The Morse code read, "Is there any hope?"

What kept these six men alive at the bottom of the sea? Why was hope the thing they inquired about when their circumstances were dire, their oxygen desperately low, and the complete darkness overwhelming?

In some proverbial sense, are we not all in a submarine 102 feet under the water? Are we not all on this planet for a limited time and tapping on the wall: Is there more? Is there hope?

Over the last year of writing this book, I chose one phrase to put in front of myself. As a writer, I like words. So, I looked for a few words to be a hook on which I could hang things. A phrase to help me keep the right perspective.

Sometimes, the best new thing is not new—it is something old that you rediscover. Like a treasure you find at the bottom of a box in your closet, you dust it off and realize, wow, I didn't know I still had that!

I wrote this phrase out on a yellow sticky note and stuck it to my laptop: *Have faith in God.*

Why these words?

I've found I don't have to make any effort to live by emotions, fear, worry, or negativity. I don't have to wake up and read:

7 keys to being selfish

10 ways to doubt yourself

21 laws of negativity

Nope. All these things come naturally to me. They are the default setting of my brain. I need to intentionally remind myself to put my eyes on God. We need to embrace faith in God. Why? Because God has everything we need to make it through the season we are in.

The narrative of our culture is tainted with negativity.

Have fear!

Have anxiety!

Have division!

Have confusion!

Don't put faith in anything or anyone—and don't dare put your actual faith in God!

But we need something more in our lives than our mind or our intellect or our logic. We need something to stir in the deeper core of our being and ignite something powerful. When I was growing up in the church as a child, there was an old-school kind of faith that dared to believe God for miracles and answers to prayer and breakthroughs. I've honestly had that faith knocked out of me at times. But I'm contending for it. Even if that means I have to write it down and put it in front of myself every day, I know I need faith in God. I know what it is to have doubts. I know what it is to feel like the obstacles in front of me are insurmountable. I've often asked, "Where do I even begin?"

What about you? Do you know that having faith in God can be a difference maker?

I want to take you deeper into the conversation of faith, because I'm not convinced that we can have a true conversation about hope without exploring the role faith plays. Hope needs faith. I would be remiss not to tell you the *full* story of where Job got his hope.

> **I'm not convinced that we can have a true conversation about hope without exploring the role faith plays. Hope needs faith.**

Historically, hope has found itself within a trio of virtues: faith, hope, and love. They are all unique and distinct virtues, yet, in a way, they are all dependent on the others. The human soul is bankrupt without the currency of hope.

I was raised in a faith tradition that had an uncomfortable relationship with pain and suffering. We were good at talking about provision and favor, but we sometimes forgot to set a seat at the table for suffering. That's why when we retold the story of Job, it had to have such a whimsical, fairy-tale ending. We didn't like dealing with the tensions—some of which, as humans, we will never be able to reconcile. The victory and breakthrough at the end needed to be presented as so awesome that it was as if the man didn't really suffer . . . cry until he had no tears . . . lose all his children . . . be so grief-stricken his friends couldn't physically recognize him.

It is faith that allows us to understand suffering. Faith is not incongruent with walking through the surprises that life throws our way. Part of the human experience has always been to ask, "Does God see? Does God care? Can God reach into my moment of need and hold my life when I can't hold it myself?"

That's why the psalmist writes, "Feel my pain and see my trouble. Forgive all my sins" (Psalm 25:18). The idea that God feels, sees, and forgives is amazing to me. My pain is not invisible to my Maker.

Whether you consider yourself a person of faith or not, no matter what you are facing right now, my wish is that you will find a lifeline that strengthens your spirit and reinvigorates your soul.

The principle of the circle

Picture your life as a circle. Imagine that everything you have full control over is in the circle, and everything you cannot control is outside the circle.

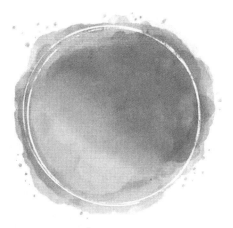

What's in your circle?

The principle of the circle is simple: most of the things we worry about we can't control. They are outside the circle.

Most of the time, we have much less control over our circumstances than we like to admit.

Can you control the decisions your children make as they grow?

Can you control the economy and how it impacts your finances?

Can you control your spouse?

Can you control your health so that you are immune from sickness?

Can you control what every other driver on the road does?

Can you control how others treat you?

We may have some minor influence over these things, but ultimately, we don't control them.

If our hope is really just a wish for constant perfect circumstances, we will live in a daily, or maybe even hourly, pendulum-like swing between euphoria and anxiety—neither of which is true hope.

Life is fragile because the future is entirely unpredictable. We have no control over what happens tomorrow. Therefore, hope for a better day is not enough to anchor our hearts.

Community and friendship help us immensely through life's challenges, but people cannot be our source of hope. No matter how gifted, educated, powerful, or wise people may be, ultimately they lack the ability to rescue us from life's valleys.

Money promises much but, in reality, does not offer unshakeable security. Billions of dollars, as so many situations have proved, cannot rescue a person from pain. No amount of property or shares of stock can bring back a loved one, restore a marriage, salvage emotions, or give us eternal security.

Circumstances

People

Money

The future

I have hope *for* all of these areas of my life, but not hope *in* them. We should all have hope *for* our circumstances and hope *for* our future. But if we deposit our faith *in* these things, we are investing in false hope. If we put our hope *in* the wrong thing, our entire stability can erode. So, while we should hope for the best in life, we need to be intentional and strategic about what we put our hope in.

Hardship reveals truth. It often exposes where our trust has been erroneously placed. Personally, I know that my own tendency is to lean toward self-sufficiency. Prudent living may stack the odds in our favor, but it doesn't give us ironclad mastery over what happens in our lives. We don't get to control life's circumstances. Nor can we control other people.

Hope in faith. Faith in God.

Circumstances change daily. Our financial security is not guaranteed. People can fail us. The future is unpredictable. I have found that if my source of hope is married to my circumstances, I will live with an underlying anxiety about the future. Often, ultimate hope cannot be *for things* but rather *in someone.* That's where faith comes in. For me, it is not about having hope *for* things. It is about who we have hope *in.* If your faith journey is completely different from mine, I want you to feel my heartfelt respect. For me, personally, putting my faith in God has helped me through my most difficult moments and seasons.

As a human race, we have a complex relationship with the lack of control we have over our story. When we add faith into the mix, sometimes it can act as a faux-control lever that we think we can use to tilt life in our favor. Faith doesn't guarantee the short-term outcome, but it makes space in the narrative of our lives for God to do surprising and wonderful things beyond what we can even understand in the moment.

I remember walking through a valley of personal discouragement. My organization had two buildings; in the same year, one was inundated with toxic water from a major flood while the other was almost completely destroyed due to a massive fire. A major flood and fire in the same year! It was millions of dollars' worth of damage.

The destruction was terrible, but I was deeply encouraged by the Psalms. This one in particular really spoke to my heart: "Why am I discouraged? Why is my heart so sad? I will put my hope in God! I will praise him again—my Savior and my God!" (Psalm 43:5). The writer is clearly walking through some kind of personal trial. In fact, they can't understand how to overcome their discouragement. They feel sadness in their heart, but the remedy seems beyond them. They have come to the end of their human ability. Now they have a choice to make: give in to negativity or put their hope in something higher. Very intentionally, they put their hope in God. I've made the same decision.

Job had to make a similar choice when the messengers informed him of his catastrophic losses. In fact, I have not yet shared with you an important detail about Job's response to losing his children. Yes, I told you that he fell to the ground for seven days and was silent, without even the breath in his lungs to grieve. But would you believe that Job worshiped God *before* his seven days of silence? He praised God (see Job 1:20–21). When Job had nothing left to hope for, his faith sustained him and eventually allowed hope to return in the subtlest of ways.

God's specialty

I wanted to look at some of the other personalities in Scripture who endured the most scandalous downfalls and the most devastating crises. The result was dramatic: I found that God *specialized* in hard situations. God is most active, most at work, most powerful, and most strategic when the odds are stacked *against* people.

Consider a few examples from Scripture:

Adam hiding in shame in a garden

Abraham leaving to a new unknown land

Moses in a desert for decades

Gideon leading a woefully outmatched army

David facing the giant Goliath

Elijah by a solitary broom tree

Jonah in a fish

Daniel in a den with lions

And ultimately Jesus on a cross

If we freeze-frame these stories at the point of pain, they seem fatal for all intents and purposes. The challenges insurmountable. The power differential too high. How could things ever turn in that person's favor? The story seemed over.

But these are the stories we most herald to communicate the nature of God toward people and to proclaim the power of hope in the fiercest storms of life. It is often in the next verse or the next chapter that we read of God's amazing hand of deliverance. Or of how God used tragedy to bring about His purpose.

If we pressed pause on your life or mine right now, it might feel similar. Is it over? Am I done? Can you ever recover? But know this—you still have another verse, another chapter, another page. God is not done yet. The story is not over. He is more at work right in this very moment than you realize.

The biblical stories of how God showed up in hopeless situations are inspiring: Noah was given blueprints for building a boat before a catastrophic storm; Joseph went from being falsely imprisoned to governor of the world's largest empire; Rahab was rescued from a life of prostitution and the destruction of her city by a scarlet rope out a window; David's family was torn apart because of his adultery, but he ruled a nation as king; Daniel was in a den with lions but didn't suffer a scratch; and, of course, Jesus rose again after the cross.

Amos 9:13 gives us this beautiful picture when it says, "'The time will come,' says the Lord, 'when the grain and grapes will grow faster than they can be harvested. Then the terraced vineyards on the hills of Israel will drip with sweet wine!'" I love the visual. A time when the vineyard of our lives will be in full bloom. The grapes are growing. Momentum and favor are flowing in our direction. Believe it in your heart—that time will come!

Unfortunately, I have this tendency to want to have all the answers . . . and *then* have faith in God. I know what it is to worry and stress about something only for God to come through and then think to myself, "I really should have more faith. But the order of the sequence matters. We need to choose faith *before* we see the answers. Faith this side of our problems. Faith in our pain. Faith in our delays. If it will make sense in hindsight, faith is what causes it to make sense right now.

One of my favorite quotes comes from Paul: "We are pressed on every side by troubles, but we are not crushed. We are perplexed, but not driven to despair. We are hunted down, but never abandoned by God. We get knocked down, but we are not destroyed" (2 Corinthians 4:8–9).

Time and again, I see examples of God at work. What has built my faith is a simple thought: if God did it for them, He can do it for me.

Sometimes, God uses extreme moments—when the odds are infinitely against us—to teach us the most profound lessons of faith. He uses the pressure of adversity to etch something of His nature into our character.

We find faith in the character of God. God is good. God is a redeemer. God is faithful.

We find faith in the promises of God. God's grace is abundant. God's peace can surpass human understanding. And God's strength is available to us all.

We find faith in the love of God. He sees our pain. He loves us unconditionally.

How large does your faith need to be in order to be effective? Jesus said it could be as small as a tiny mustard seed. Faith can be microscopic; it can start in deeply broken and painful situations or in a haze of doubt. But large doors swing on small hinges, and the smallest measure of faith can open huge opportunities for God to move in your life.

Let us now return to the story of the S-4 submarine. The rescue team did everything humanly possible, but they faced a race against time, hazardous conditions, and primitive technology. Despite valiant efforts, the remaining six men passed away.

The media around the world celebrated the heroism of those who attempted rescues and the illuminating hope of those trapped. In the passing days, the families of the lost gathered to celebrate their lives.

In the courtyard of St. Mary of the Harbor Episcopal Church, they congregated around a wooden cross made from driftwood.[2] I can picture them—weeping, grief-stricken—and in the middle stood the wooden cross.

In my mind, the cross in that courtyard was much more than ornamental because it symbolized an imperative message: when hope doesn't give you the outcome you need, grab on to faith! There is no more universally recognized symbol of the hope that comes from suffering than the cross of Christ. When life goes from smooth sailing to a grief-stricken church courtyard, there must always be a cross in the middle!

Do you feel the ache of loneliness? Has daily life lost its joy? Have anxiety and depression become your companions?

Are circumstances overwhelming you? If you answered yes to any of these questions, be encouraged—for you are simply positioned as the perfect candidate to receive the hope that comes from God. It's never too late to discover faith.

Faith. Hope. Love.

We have hope because we are loved.

Three things will last forever—faith, hope, and love—and the greatest of these is love.

—1 Corinthians 13:13

CHAPTER 11

Eden

See life through an eternal scope

IN NEW YORK CITY sits the United States National Debt Clock. The sign displays a real-time calculation of the spiraling debt, which is well over $30 trillion. Every second, the number ticks upward.

The original clock was created by Seymour Durst in 1989. Today, most people walk by too focused on their own personal challenges to pay much attention to it. But this real-time calculation of national debt should cause people to be alarmed, to stop and consider the big picture: one day, this debt must be addressed.

In similar ways, our minds and hearts are often distracted by the day-to-day challenges we face. But there *is* a clock over our lives. It is inevitable. It is unavoidable. It is the countdown of our days.

What if our ability to flourish in our lives today is intrinsically linked to what comes next?

It's like knowing the ending of a movie before you watch it. The climactic scene may be full of tension—a car chase, a twist in a murder mystery, or a breakup—but you don't get too caught up in the emotion of the moment if you already know that the main character triumphs at the end.

You might be enduring pain now that's like a scene out of a movie. Know this, though: at the end, you escape from your ropes, untie your friend, and jump from the burning ship,

167

all while getting the bad guy. The timeline of your victory may not be here and now, but you have the most incredible triumph to look forward to.

The conclusion gives us the peace we need for the scene we are living now. If we know how the story ends, it changes how we experience the journey. What happens next is so wonderful and incredible that it can be carried with us now.

I want to say five definitive things to you in this chapter that have the potential to change everything about your life.

1. Hope has a time

Despite our advances in medicine and technology, humanity's mortality rate remains at one hundred percent. (Yes, I know it seems out of place to write that we are all going to die in a book about hope!) Yet, one of the touchstone concepts for understanding life is that none of us lives forever on earth. A famous psalm reads,

> LORD, remind me how brief my time on earth will be. Remind me that my days are numbered—how fleeting my life is. You have made my life no longer than the width of my hand. My entire lifetime is just a moment to you; at best, each of us is but a breath.
>
> Psalm 39:4–5

Hold up your hand and measure the width—that's your life. Breathe one breath and see how long it lasts—that's your timeline. Hope must be connected to more than circumstances and troubles that resolve themselves here and now. If we measure life based on the time on our wristwatch, we will often struggle to live with hope. There is another clock we can look to that gives us a better measure of our lives: the clock of eternity.

Hold up your hand and measure the width—that's your life. Breathe one breath and see how long it lasts—that's your timeline.

The time zone of hope is eternity; if we adjust our personal clocks to synchronize with heaven's clock, we will see things on earth very differently. Eternity should be the scope we measure things by. It gives new context to pain, loss, and ultimately even death. An eternal mindset is not just about life at the end of our days on earth, but rather it's about giving us a new context for how to live our lives *now*. If we gauge life by our earthly increments of minutes, hours, days, and years, we will perpetually struggle to maintain our hope. But beginning to see things through the lens of an eternal scope can alter the way we view every storm and hardship.

2. Hope has an origin

In the biblical narrative, the story of humanity starts in a garden called Eden. Eden was a paradise so magnificent that it is beyond comprehension. Lush trees, rivers, pristine nature. There was no death, no anguish, no crime, no sorrow. It was the way God intended it—a paradise where people would live forever.

But the first family made some poor decisions, so darkness swept over humanity. Paradise was shattered. The thorny vines of murder, pain, and everything ugly began to grow and spread.

There was something about that original Eden that serves as more than a history lesson: it gives us a glimpse of the future. God never gave up on His plan of Eden—a paradise, a family, a community. And, in some deep ways, our hearts long for what was originally lost: a place of complete joy, with no sadness or wounds.

Eden is the earliest picture of hope. It is the counterweight to what is to come. Eden is a whisper of heaven. Tolkien saw this connection between Eden and our ultimate hope: "We all long for [Eden], and we are constantly glimpsing it: our whole nature at its best and least corrupted, its gentlest and most humane, is still soaked with the sense of 'exile.'"[1]

The idea of Eden being connected to our future paradise is symbolized in the onyx stone. In Eden, there was a rare mineral called onyx (see Ezekiel 28:13). It is interesting that, later in human history, Hebrew priests would wear onyx stones on their shoulders as they stood before the people (see Exodus 28:9–12). The stone was a visual reminder of the origin of hope, a representation of a place where one's deepest dreams and aspirations for a life of wholeness, happiness, and love can exist.

Onyx was not used to remind people of what had been lost, nor as a provocation as if saying, "Humanity used to live in paradise with no suffering or storms." Rather, this onyx was a symbol of a promise—a physical signpost—that, in the middle of our broken human condition, God had not forgotten His original plan of paradise. Onyx is also mentioned later, in John's vision of heaven (see Revelation 21:19–20).

Eden: a visual cue for broken humanity. Heaven: the symmetrical image of a greater plan of redemption. The two bookends of humanity.

Eden is the first picture of a world of hope, and it points us toward our future—a new paradise with no sorrow or death.

3. Hope has a home

What did Job know that we also need to know in order to have the same brand of remarkable hope?

Job said these words: "As for me, I know that my Redeemer lives, and he will stand upon the earth at last" (Job 19:25). When Job lost everything, one of the truths that kept him alive was his belief that this earth will eventually be fixed and all pain will be erased.

This earth is broken, but it is not the final chapter. God has not given up on His original plan—first seen in Eden—for humanity to live with complete joy. God has a master plan to change things: He will create a new earth, and we can live in paradise forever (see Isaiah 65:17; Isaiah 66:22; 2 Peter 3:13; and Revelation 21:1).

My favorite word that describes heaven is *home* (see Ezekiel 37:27). To me, home speaks of family, love, and warmth. In fact, Jesus said that the antidote to a troubled heart is to know that a home awaits us in heaven (see John 14:1–4).

Knowing about this final home is like having GPS coordinates. I am often guilty of getting into my car and just driving, thinking I know my city well enough to find my destination. It's only when I end up on a dirt road in a remote area with long grass and a faded timber fence that I realize I am lost. A journey with no destination is frustrating and confusing.

Have you ever wondered, "How did my life end up here?" Job had the coordinates of his eternal home entered in his heart.

The coordinates give us an end destination, but they also change how we navigate the turns and roadblocks along the way. When we know where we are heading, it influences the entire way we approach the journey. Basketball superstar Stephen Curry said, "I know I have a place in heaven waiting for me because of Him, and that's something no earthly prize or trophy could ever top."[2] Knowing about our ultimate home gives us a new perspective now. Scripture invites us to be reassured "because of the hope laid up for you in heaven" (Colossians 1:5 ESV).

There is "feeling hopeful," and then there is *ultimate hope*. Resilience. Encouragement. Friendship. Mindfulness. All of these may add to a feeling of hopefulness in the moment. But ultimate hope is something much different. Ultimate hope is not just more hope on top of hopefulness—the way one would add another shovel of soil to an already large dirt pile. Ultimate hope is a different species.

Ultimate hope is not found when we understand why we are suffering. Ultimate hope is not found in a friend, good advice, or a new technique. Ultimate hope has less to do with how we feel or what our circumstances present to us, and more to do with the big questions of life. Our life needs the precise GPS coordinates. Our final home. Our ultimate hope. Our new Eden. Our ultimate hope is that heaven exists.

4. Hope has a name

Many years after the life of Job, there was another man in the narrative of Scripture named Jesus, who shared many of the same qualities. Like Job, Jesus was good and blameless before God. Like Job, raiders came and brought pain to His life. But what makes Jesus's life different from Job's is how it ended—in total victory, and that victory is significant for us.

In fact, Tolkien, our good catastrophe friend, saw in Jesus the clearest example of his concept that the greatest good can come out of the greatest crises. Tolkien writes, "The birth of Christ is the eucatastrophe of man's history."[3] Jesus was like Job, but even better than Job because He offers a life of hope to all. One of the most compelling Scriptures about Jesus reads, "And his name will be the hope of all the world" (Matthew 12:21). Indeed, it is the name of Jesus that has brought and still brings hope to generations of people around the world.

What did Jesus say about life?

Just before His time on earth ended, Jesus spoke to His closest friends about eternity. He left them with these words: "I have told you these things, so that in me you may have peace. In this world you will have trouble. But take heart! I have overcome the world" (John 16:33 NIV).

In this world, you will have trouble. It's a statement that feels brooding. Clouds are forming on the horizon of your life. You can't outrun or escape it. This thing called trouble will interrupt your life. We are not given any indication about how to know when trouble is coming, nor how it will turn up. We are just promised that it will visit our lives.

Jesus was candid: He knew that life has unavoidable troubles and that we all come to a point where life hurts. But He made the claim that you can still have peace amid the challenges. This kind of peace is an inner calm and an overall wellness, regardless of circumstances. We often see

> Hope is more than a feeling, a virtue, or an outlook. Hope is a person, and hope has a name: Jesus.

peace as an end to all the world's problems. Yet, Jesus defined peace as something that starts in our hearts. It is only from internal peace that outward peace becomes a reality.

Jesus's ultimate claim about the solution to our troubles is captured in His use of the word *overcome*. Linguistic experts tell us that the original Greek word for overcome in John 16:33 is from the root word *nike*. This word denotes a sense of victory—winning in the face of obstacles. It existed long before a sporting goods company chose it as a name. Jesus teaches that we can have hope in the eternal life that only He offers.

Hope is more than a feeling, a virtue, or an outlook. Hope is a person, and hope has a name: Jesus.

5. Hope has an invitation

Along our life journeys, we all experience situations that cause hope to shift from being a luxury to a lifeline. Hope suddenly becomes a *now* word. No matter how great our education, wealth, or connections, we all reach a point where we exhaust the resources available to us. We discover the cold reality that our strength is not limitless. Eugene Peterson writes, "The single qualification for being eligible for God's help is that we be in trouble."[4] I've come to realize that, at one point or another, we are all in a form of trouble—which means we all qualify for the invitation of help.

The question is this: Where do we turn when there is nowhere else to go? When we are down and out, messed up, fearful, and stressed, to whom do we look? When bankruptcy brings us to our knees, when the death of a loved one takes our joy away, or when our errors in judgment shipwreck our lives, how do we dig ourselves out of the difficulties we find ourselves in?

An eternal view is what puts our earthly challenges into perspective, which is why 2 Corinthians 4:17 (NIV) says, "For our light and momentary troubles are achieving for us an eternal glory that far outweighs them all." I've come to understand my story within the larger narrative of humanity. Stress doesn't win. Violence doesn't win. Failure doesn't win. Cancer doesn't win. Even death doesn't win. Knowing that the end of this life on earth is a comma, not a period, and that we have an eternal home gives me peace within the drama of life.

Jesus made the ultimate invitation to all of us: "Come to me, all of you who are weary and carry heavy burdens, and I will give you rest" (Matthew 11:28). We all come to a place where we are weary and carrying burdens. Jesus offers an invitation to live life, to experience joy, to dream again. It is an invitation to eternity. An invitation for the dead stump to flourish and come back to life.

The invitation is to all of humanity. It is to you.

Tears

I was raised in simpler times. No internet. No mobile devices. No social media. My childhood memories consist of riding a BMX bicycle around the neighborhood, playing basketball at the local park, and competing with my brothers over virtually everything, including how much cereal we could eat in the morning.

I got married at nineteen and moved from Australia to the West Coast of the United States. I traveled the world. Went to college. Launched my career.

When I became a parent, the subjects of pain, adversity, and hope became much more real and personal. While every paternal instinct in me tries to shield my sons from hardship, I know that everyone experiences pain in life.

My youngest son broke his arm when he was five years old. After he had been to the hospital, I told him how brave he was. He replied, "Dad, I am so brave, only one tear fell from my face." I thought it was cute and used it as an opportunity to tell him that even brave people cry, and that tears show that we are human.

Our suffering in life is what makes the ultimate claim about heaven so captivating. It is described as a place where God will wipe every tear from our eyes, a place with no death, no sorrow, and no pain (see Revelation 21:4).

We all cry at times, but is there more to tears than we realize? That's a question Rose-Lynn Fisher set out to answer in her book *The Topography of Tears*. She shared, "Eventually, I started wondering—would a tear of grief look any different than a tear of joy? And how would they compare to, say, an onion tear?"[5]

For more than eight years, Fisher studied the salt crystals from dried tears on glass slides. With a microscope and camera, she photographed the crystalline patterns of the full range of human emotion: grief, sorrow, laughter, elation. The artistic results are stunning and moving.

The crystal patterns from tears of grief are sparse and barren, with sharp edges. The crystals from tears of laughter are round, uncontained, and fluid. The patterns from tears that were the result of major life change appear dense, almost layered on top of each other in confusion. When I looked at the images, it seemed to me that our tears carry emotion and expression. Fisher calls the photographs of tears "aerial views of emotional terrain. . . . Each one of our tears carries a microcosm of the collective human experience."[6]

Nothing else captures hardship in life like tears. Tears depict the pain of humanity. The promise, however, of every tear being wiped from our eyes is deeply significant. More than simple comfort, it is a promise that the very source of our pain and adversity will be completely removed. One of my favorite psalms puts it this way: "You keep track of all my sorrows. You have collected all my tears in your bottle. You have recorded each one in your book" (Psalm 56:8). The picture of every tear being collected in a bottle is not a promise that we will never endure pain in our lifetimes, nor can we comprehend, as humans, why an all-powerful God would allow pain in the first place. But what we are promised is that God sees and God cares.

The spiritual toll of suffering

Suffering is never merely circumstantial. Its roots run deep. Something happens—something bad, something unexpected. Something we wish we never would have had to face. The vine of suffering soon grows. It travels up the wall of our everyday life, and it finds its way inside the home of our soul. It is there, in the very depths of our inner world, that suffering attempts to suffocate our being.

Suffering affects our inner world. It may start as cancer in a loved one, or a drug-addicted adolescent, or debts that cannot be repaid. But we must realize that it never stops there. Naturally, suffering travels with questions: Why is this happening? Where is God? Is this my fault? Why me? If there is a beautiful mind at work in the universe, why is there an ugliness that tarnishes our lives? These questions are no longer about the marriage, or the child, or money. They become questions about life, questions about God. Measured on a long-enough timeline, suffering can alter and change the very essence of who we are.

We can never win the battle for hope if we don't identify the larger war we have to fight—the one within our soul. We do a disservice to our treatment of hope if we reserve our conversation for the world of practical habits or easy-to-find solutions. You and I have an inner life. In Job's era, that inner life was referred to as the heart. It meant much more than a physical organ; it referred to the very center of a person. It's more than our mind or our thoughts, though it may include those things. It's the sum of our mind, our will, and our emotions. History has shown us that while the physical body can be easily broken, this "heart" can show resilience that defies all logic. If I can win the battle between suffering and hope in my heart, then I can do the same in my everyday life.

Sometimes when people experience pain, they make decisions they would never have made otherwise. They face the temptation of turning away from their convictions. They wrestle with thoughts and ideas they never had until the storm hit. They find doubts, which had been dormant seeds, sprouting and growing stronger. Even their faith can start to crack and give way. Virtues such as kindness and peace succumb to anger, resentment, and even hate. Discouragement. Confusion fogs their vision.

Hope at a heart level, a spiritual level, is transformative to the human experience. What a paradox! Suffering can deepen, strengthen, and enrich your inner world, and actually amplify the inner story of hope. The same suffering that brings a dark ugliness to some people's souls can, for others, produce a captivating beauty.

Our person of interest, Job, has some inspired moments. But let's be candid: Job also went on to accuse God of destroying him and grinding his life into a powder. There were times when Job focused his rage and heartache on God. Job spent a lot of time ranting at God and asking questions of heaven. It's interesting that God doesn't seem to answer the questions Job asks. God responds from a completely different vantage point. He never really gives Job a direct answer as to why he suffered. No clear, quotable phrase is available to neatly wrap up the story. Yet, God does speak. He responds to the pain Job is experiencing. God seems to point to himself as some form of ultimate answer. God doesn't offer further information about why Job experienced such bitter devastation—rather, God talked about His own character and virtue. One way of seeing it is that God was presenting himself as the answer to life's pain. A promise that we are loved, valued, seen, and heard, and that we are not alone on this planet. It reminds us that, amid the dramas of all of our lives, the grand arc of history is bending toward a master plan: God's ultimate redemption of humanity.

When we can't understand *what* is happening in life, there is a *who* we can put our trust in: God. You are not alone. You are loved. You are seen. Every tear has been recorded.

Can you even imagine a life with no sorrow, pain, or loss of any kind? Can a place so wonderful be possible? Hope points us toward the ultimate solution, the ultimate victory, the ultimate happiness: heaven.

If there is no pain in heaven, it means that there will be no children's hospitals, no refugee camps, no human trafficking, no racism, no physical pain of any kind, no hurt or arguments, no stress or anxiety.

And no more tears.

✳ ✳ ✳

While writing this book, my brother's cancer journey came to an end. He passed away at the age of forty-one.

Being only eighteen months apart in age meant he was often the only one present to witness so many formative moments in my life. It feels like I have lost part of me.

On the day I found out about my brother's death, I was in Boston, Massachusetts. I walked down to the waterfront overlooking the Charles River to try to clear my mind and comprehend what had happened. As I looked out across the water, my eyes were drawn to the scores of little sailboats on the river. White and red sails. They darted and danced with the wind. Zigging and zagging. And yet as all these little sailboats turned and bobbed on the river, they collectively created a sense of serenity, not chaos.

It caused me to reflect on life. Ultimately our lives are like those sailboats. We don't traverse a predetermined path. Our lives don't unfold in clean linear lines. Within all the adventures and surprises of life—and as we hold on for dear life and do our best to orient our sails to the wind—there is a bigger picture. There is a big story that holds all of our little stories.

This is why having a worldview of *ultimate* hope matters so much. Ultimate hope is there when we don't get answers and solutions to our present challenges. Ultimate hope provides me the comfort and perspective that one day I will be reunited with my brother. An understanding that heaven is real is not just a nice thought. There's really no other way to have ultimate hope.

I have come home at last! This is my real country! I belong here. This is the land I have been looking for all my life, though I never knew it till now.

—C. S. Lewis[1]

Cherry Blossoms

The hope framework

I'VE TRAVELED to the South Island of New Zealand to write these final thoughts. It's here that the writings of Tolkien were brought to life in blockbuster movies. It is the last few days of winter now; the air is crisp, the primordial-looking alpine mountains are visible and still tipped with snow, but spring is already breaking forth. The aqua-blue waterfront of Queenstown is coming alive with stunning cherry blossoms, one of my favorite trees. Their spring bloom has arrived early with bright pink flowers. In Japan, the cherry blossom is sacred, its flowers emblematic of the fragility and shortness of life.

Before a flower blooms from the barren branches of winter, it has been forming in a bud for months. Hope had always been there; it just hadn't made itself public yet.

Looking at these cherry blossoms brings me back to how we started: considering a tree that had been cut down to a stump and needed only the scent of water to come back to life. Could it be that the scent of hope is powerful enough to bring our lives back into bloom, even when they have been cut down?

The bright pink flowers make me think of Job's life flourishing after he lost everything. As I look up at the mountains, I am reminded of Tolkien's eucatastrophe. It feels like, in this one scene, everything is coming full circle. No matter how cold and dark the winter, spring can never be contained. New life is always a more potent force than pain.

Think for a moment of the idea of what cherry blossoms represent: fragility. I've often struggled with just how fragile life feels. I've wondered, "How can I have confidence when it feels like the world is rapidly changing?" I can't control the macro changes happening in nations and economies. I also can't control the micro changes of shifting circumstances in my own home. Is it possible to have confidence amid the fragility of life?

Could it be that the scent of hope is powerful enough to bring our lives back into bloom, even when they have been cut down?

The book of Job speaks to this when it reads, "Their confidence hangs by a thread. They are leaning on a spider's web" (Job 8:14).

I hate spiders—let's be honest, none of us really like them. But when I think of the metaphor of my life leaning on a spider's web, it is a picture of having confidence in the wrong things. No spider builds its web to last forever. They are not engineered to bear structural loads. They are temporary. At any point, a web could give. They were never designed to be a support structure.

The picture is a warning not to put our confidence in things that aren't strong enough to hold us up when storms hit!

We all have "spiderwebs." In other words, we put our confidence in things like money, technology, achievements, and even people. All good things, but let's face it: they are spiderwebs—they can't hold up our lives!

Life is fragile. So let's not lean our lives on spiderwebs. Instead, let's learn how to build our lives with a confident hope in God that can exist within the fragility of our world.

Broken hope

Job was not afraid to ask the big questions of life. When his life was hit with dark tragedy, he asked, "Where then is my hope? Can anyone find it?" (Job 17:15). You may be in a similar place in your own journey right now, asking if any hope is available.

I think Job broke the version of hope that is reliant on every circumstance in life being perfect and pain-free. Outcome-based hope is the fantasy of a life without troubles. What Job lost was real. It was irreplaceable. But Job sketched a new picture of hope—a hope made for moments when circumstances *don't* improve. A hope so incandescent it can illuminate the darkest nights. A hope so buoyant it can bob to the surface amid the most devastating floods. It's a hope that is, in fact, oxygen for the human soul—the ability to grow, thrive, and dream within imperfection.

The hope Job broke works only in green pastures, on sunny days, and in perfect times.

The true hope Job demonstrated is available when cancer attacks, divorce divides, or the stress of the daily grind feels like too much. Hope lives in trauma, adversity, and valleys of discouragement.

We use the phrase "thorn in the flesh" to describe a persistent problem we can't seem to solve. But the wording originates in the New Testament writings of Paul, who wrote about a thorn in his flesh and how he prayed three times for it to be removed. Surprisingly, God didn't remove it. As a missionary, Paul had devoted his life to serving God and had experienced extreme suffering. Surely God would grant him this one small request! But God, for whatever reason, declined. And the answer Paul received from God is what I find to be one of the most beautiful pieces of prose in ancient literature:

> Each time he said, "My grace is all you need. My power works best in weakness." So now I am glad to boast about my weaknesses, so that the power of Christ can work through me. That's why I take pleasure in my weaknesses, and in the insults, hardships, persecutions, and troubles that I suffer for Christ. For when I am weak, then I am strong.
>
> 2 Corinthians 12:9–10

Paul was able to piece it all together—his weaknesses and insults and hardships—and see them as earthly discomforts that made him look to God for strength. We all have thorns. They are neither comfortable nor pleasant. But they can push us toward hope. In doing so, they offer us a service. A benefit. They assist us. For in finding hope, we find one of life's true treasure troves.

As I've traveled through my life, I've found that hardship has been a constant companion. When I was a teenager, I assumed that my identity would be shaped mostly by what vocation I chose. However, I've come to realize that my pain has marked me as much, if not more, as my achievements or successes. Pain does something to the center of who we are. I've felt alone. Felt broken. Felt lost. And I've also seen how, in my moments of greatest adversity, a brilliant ray of sunshine has somehow penetrated the darkest of cloud cover.

Everything can be traced back to one idea: hope can germinate only in the heat of the fires of life.

Hope is humanity's universal need. It crosses cultures and nations. It is sought by the rich and the poor, by the young and the old. Every person on earth needs hope.

Perhaps, right now, you are trying to survive the death of a spouse or child, mental health challenges, or a serious sickness. These can rip and tear at the very fiber of our soul, as if something deep inside is being broken that can never be glued back together.

The human soul cannot live without hope. It can thrive neither on cliché hope nor on the abandonment of all hope. It needs real hope. And real hope, when defined and practiced, is more powerful than I ever imagined. It is a treasure that has enabled generations of people to thrive in adversity.

Allow yourself to hope

I got up to watch the sunrise over the ocean today. It was unashamedly majestic. The burst of gold rays pierced the darkness of dawn. There was a visual disregard for all the hurt, loss, and tragedy that yesterday brought. The sun didn't arrive timid, tiptoeing on eggshells. It did not nervously inquire, "I know yesterday was hard, so is it okay if I shine just one little, tiny ray today?" No. The sun arrived with unrestrained glory and brilliance. It filled the entire sky.

Every mountain, sea, field, valley, and home was flooded with light. Was the sun unaware of every tragedy that occurred yesterday? Every death? Every sickness? Every loss? If it did know, would it not hold off for a few hours?

Yet, the sun shows up. Every. Single. Day.

Is there truly any better picture of hope than sunrise? Yes, the night has been dark. But darkness is not the end of the human experience. There is always light. And when hope is unleashed, it floods every part of our lives, just like the sun.

It struck me, as my face glowed with the arrival of a new day, that the sun *warmed*. The sunrise brought a healing quality—this warmth I am referencing—that carried a positive energy. And I think that's what hope is. It's not so garish and offensive that we need to pretend we have no problems, no worries, no obstacles. But as we live within those circumstances and challenges, hope brings a warmth to the soul.

We need not be afraid or cautious of hope in the same way we need not be afraid or cautious of the sun rising.

What if hope never meant a life that was trouble free, and what if it didn't promise a future of perfect circumstances? This atypical version of hope is engineered for adversity. While it doesn't always wave away our difficulties with a magic wand, you will discover it does something infinitely greater: it changes us. It *makes* us.

We are supposed to be more than our brokenness. Life is meant to be more than our pain. We must become attuned to spotting the specks of light that are breaking through.

Sure, at times hope may present itself as an emotion that wells up from our souls. We can feel it with each heartbeat. But while this is the familiar way of seeing hope—an emotion—hope can also come dressed as a decision. Hope

. . . a decision? I know it may sound a bit clinical, a little forced. Yet, I think it is an important part of the personality of hope. We can decide to hope. In fact, we can decide to hope even when the normal entourage that travels with hope stays at home. Even when our circumstances present no supporting evidence, we can *choose* hope.

To hope is to be human. When you hope, hope big, hope boldly, hope dangerously. Hope with the understanding that hope itself is a force, a medicine, and an agent of change.

Your anticipation of the future influences what tomorrow brings.

You can't half hope any more than you can half jump into a swimming pool. Commit. Leap into the deep. Real hope cannot be exaggerated or overpromised, for while our circumstances in life may change, hope remains steady. It is a life source that is absolutely fundamental to our existence. Hope is certainly a better way to live than panic and fear.

> **To hope is to be human. When you hope, hope big, hope boldly, hope dangerously. Hope with the understanding that hope itself is a force, a medicine, and an agent of change.**

There's light at the end of the tunnel. You can weather the storm, walk through the valley, and hold on during the midnight hour. A new horizon awaits you, and your first step on this new path of your life journey starts right now.

The clouds will soon pass. A new chapter is yet to be written. Breathe deeply and allow hope to enter your soul one more time. Pick yourself up and dust yourself off. You're not done yet! You can make it. You *will* make it. You are a remarkably resilient person.

Do something that brings you joy. Hike up a mountain and watch the sunset. Go camping and toast marshmallows over a smoky fire. Play your favorite board game with friends. Take a barefoot walk in the shallow waves of the beach at dusk.

You can breathe again. You can dream again. You can laugh again. Maybe, just maybe, your future is greater than your past, your best moments are ahead, and the next chapter will be your best yet.

Hope Framework

Let's bring it all together.

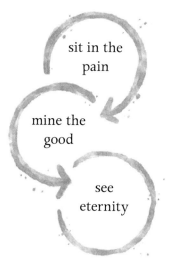

Sit in the pain.

- Don't sanitize the mess.
- Hope needs human skin.

Mine the good.

- See the eucatastrophes—the greatest good comes from the greatest pain.
- Embrace everyday moments.
- Overcome anxiety.
- Forge purpose from your pain.

See eternity.

- Expect new life to grow.
- See beyond the storms.
- Find faith in your pain.

Job's poetic claim that a stump can flourish and begin life anew at the scent of water captivated me. Expect good things. Anticipate divine reversals. Lean into optimism. Embrace light. Look up and feel the warmth of the sun. The dark velvet of night is being pulled back. The hour before dawn is the darkest hour, so hold on. The sun is about to rise!

Our ultimate hope is found in this timeless message: "And his name will be the hope of all the world" (Matthew 12:21).

At the scent of water, a stump can grow again. And, with even the smallest measure of hope, your life will flourish abundantly once more.

Darkness must pass

A new day will come

And when the sun shines

It will shine out the clearer.

—J. R. R. Tolkien[1]

Notes

Chapter 1: Stumptown

1. Elisabeth Elliot, *Suffering is Never for Nothing* (Nashville: B&H Books, 2019).

2. Jess Reid, "Study Reveals Plants 'Listen' to Find Sources of Water," *The University of Western Australia*, April 11, 2017, http://www.news.uwa.edu.au/201704119544/research/study-reveals-plants-listen-find-sources-water.

Chapter 2: Saint Anne

1. J. Cole, "Intro," Recorded May 2007, By Any Means, digital download.

Chapter 3: Eucatastrophe

1. C. S. Lewis, *The Problem of Pain* (New York: HarperOne, 2001).

2. J. R. R. Tolkien to Priscilla Tolkien, November 26, 1963, Tolkien Estate, https://www.tolkienestate.com/letters/priscilla-tolkien-26-nov-1963/.

3. J. R. R. Tolkien, "On Fairy-Stories," *Essays Presented to Charles Williams*, ed. C. S. Lewis (Grand Rapids, MI: Eerdmans, 1966), 90–105.

4. Thanks to Jason G. Duesing for context on Tolkien's early use of *eucatastrophe*. Jason G. Duesing, *Mere Hope: Life in an Age of Cynicism* (Nashville: B&H Books, 2018), loc. 1183, Kindle.

5. J. R. R. Tolkien, *The Letters of J. R. R. Tolkien*, ed. Humphrey Carpenter with Christopher Tolkien (Boston: Houghton Mifflin Harcourt, 2000), 100.

6. Steve Jobs, commencement address, June 12, 2005, Stanford University, https://news.stanford.edu/2005/06/14/jobs-061505/.

7. Mara Reinstein, "'I Wasn't Very Good!' Jerry Seinfeld Reflects on his Early Routines, Favorite Seinfeld Episode and the Future of Comedy," *Parade*, October 2, 2020, https://parade.com/1096425/maramovies/jerry-seinfeld-is-this-anything/.

Chapter 4: Backyard Basketball

1. Nicholas Sparks, *A Walk to Remember* (New York: Grand Central, 2001).
2. Jonathan Givony, "NCAA Weekly Performers, 2/28/09," *DraftExpress*, http://www.draftexpress.com/article/NCAA-Weekly-Performers-22809 -3122/. Quoted in Erik Malinowski, *Betaball: How Silicon Valley and Science Built One of the Greatest Basketball Teams in History* (New York: Atria Books, 2017), 40.
3. David Fleming, "Stephen Curry: The Full Circle," *ESPN*, April 23, 2015, https://abc7news.com/sports/stephen-curry-the-full-circle/678281/. Quoted in Clayton Geoffreys, *Stephen Curry: The Inspiring Story of One of Basketball's Sharpest Shooters* (Winter Park, FL: Calvintir Books, LLC, 2014), 8.

Chapter 5: Broken Pianos

1. Susan Cain, *Bittersweet* (New York: Crown, 2022), xxv.
2. Timothy Keller, *Walking with God through Pain and Suffering* (London: Hodder & Stoughton, 2013), loc. 216, Kindle.

Chapter 6: Storms, Shipwrecks, Serpents

1. Leigh Sales, *Any Ordinary Day: Blindsides, Resilience and What Happens After the Worst Day of Your Life* (London: Penguin Books, 2018), 1.
2. Liz Mineo, "Good Genes Are Nice, but Joy Is Better," *The Harvard Gazette*, April 11, 2017, https://news.harvard.edu/gazette/story/2017/04/over -nearly-80-years-harvard-study-has-been-showing-how-to-live-a-healthy-and -happy-life/.
3. Mineo, "Good Genes Are Nice, but Joy Is Better."
4. Christopher G. De Pree, *Physics Made Simple: A Complete Introduction to the Basic Principles of This Fundamental Science* (New York: Crown, 2010), Kindle.

Chapter 7: Tightrope

1. Bill Gates, "This Animal Kills More People in a Day than Sharks Do in a Century," *Gates Notes*, April 23, 2018, https://www.gatesnotes.com /Health/Mosquito-Week-2018.
2. Jerry Weissman, "Another Humorous View on the Fear of Public Speaking," *Forbes*, June 17, 2014, https://www.forbes.com/sites/jerryweissman /2014/06/17/another-humorous-view-on-the-fear-of-public-speaking/#1ec 544367081.
3. Benson-Henry Institute, "Mission and History," https://bensonhenry institute.org/mission-history/.

4. Nelson Mandela, *Long Walk to Freedom: The Autobiography of Nelson Mandela* (London: Abacus, 1994), 622.

5. Martin Seligman, *The Hope Circuit: A Psychologist's Journey from Helplessness to Optimism* (New York: Public Affairs, 2018), 213.

6. Julie K. Norem, "Defensive Pessimism, Anxiety, and the Complexity of Evaluating Self-Regulation," *Social and Personality Psychology Compass*, 2, no. 1 (January 2008): 121–34, https://doi.org/10.1111/j.1751-9004.2007 .00053.x.

7. Seligman, *The Hope Circuit*, 70.

Chapter 8: 200 Hands

1. David Kinnaman, foreword to *The Loneliness Epidemic: Why So Many of Us Feel Alone—and How Leaders Can Respond*, by Susan Mettes (Grand Rapids: Brazos, 2021), x.

2. Brian Resnick, "22 Percent of Millennials Say They Have 'No Friends,'" *Vox*, August 1, 2019, https://www.vox.com/science-and-health/2019/8/1 /20750047/millennials-poll-loneliness.

3. Sian Leah Beilock, "Why Young Americans Are Lonely," *Scientific American*, July 27, 2020, https://www.scientificamerican.com/article/why -young-americans-are-lonely/.

4. Jennie Allen, *Find Your People: Building Deep Community in a Lonely World* (Colorado Springs: WaterBrook, 2022), 7.

5. "The True Friend Walks In When Others Walk Out," *Quote Investigator*, May 7, 2019, https://quoteinvestigator.com/2019/05/07/friend-walk/.

6. Eddie Jaku, *The Happiest Man on Earth* (Sydney: Macmillan Australia, 2020), 59.

7. Robert Waldinger, "What Makes a Good Life? Lessons From the Longest Study on Happiness," December 2015, TEDxBeaconStreet, https://www .ted.com/talks/robert_waldinger_what_makes_a_good_life_lessons_from _the_longest_study_on_happiness/transcript?language=en.

8. Joe Albright, "Draw Your Circle Bigger," *DialHope*, November 7, 2016, https://www.dialhope.org/draw-circle-bigger/.

Chapter 9: Watchmaker

1. Mary Schmich, "Advice, Like Youth, Probably Just Wasted on the Young," *Chicago Tribune* (Chicago, IL), June 1, 1997.

2. "Resilient," *Macmillan Dictionary Blog*, http://www.macmillandiction aryblog.com/resilient.

3. Rolex, "Perpetual Movements: Rolex Watchmaking," accessed January 7, 2021, https://www.rolex.com/watches/rolex-watchmaking/new-calibre -3255.html.

4. Meg Jay, *Supernormal: Childhood Adversity and the Untold Story of Resilience* (New York: Twelve Books, 2017), 56–57.

5. Pauline Ladiges, "The story of our eucalypts," *Australian Academy of Science*, accessed January 7, 2021, https://www.science.org.au/curious/earth -environment/story-our-eucalypts.

6. Matthew McConaughey, *Greenlights* (London: Headline Books, 2020), 14.

Chapter 10: Submarine

1. McConaughey, *Greenlights*.

2. Joseph A. Williams, *Seventeen Fathoms Deep: The Saga of the Submarine S-4 Disaster* (Chicago: Chicago Review Press, 2015), 260.

Chapter 11: Eden

1. J. R. R. Tolkien, *The Letters of J. R. R. Tolkien*, ed. Humphrey Carpenter with Christopher Tolkien (Boston: Houghton Mifflin Harcourt, 2000), 110.

2. Stephen Curry, "Stephen Curry: In My Own Words," *FCA Magazine*, June 17, 2015, https://www.fca.org/magazine-story/2015/06/17/curry-in-his -own-words.

3. J. R. R. Tolkien, *Tree and Leaf: Including "Mythopoeia"* (New York: HarperCollins, 2012), loc. 905, Kindle.

4. Eugene Peterson, "Eligible for God's Help," September 18, 2019, *The Message Devotional Bible*, https://messagebible.com/eligible-for-gods-help/.

5. Joshua Filmer, "Human Tears Under a Microscope," *Futurism*, July 26, 2014, https://futurism.com/human-tears-under-a-microscope.

6. Rose-Lynn Fisher, *The Topography of Tears* (New York: Bellevue Literary Press, 2017), 6–7.

Chapter 12: Cherry Blossoms

1. C.S. Lewis, *The Last Battle* (New York: HarperCollins, 2002).

In Honor Of

1. J. R. R. Tolkien, *The Lord of the Rings: The Two Towers* (Boston: Houghton Mifflin, 1982).

Benjamin Windle is an innovative and empathetic author and speaker. As a pastor for over 20 years, he's walked with many people through the dark shadows and valleys of the human experience. He has dedicated his life to helping people overcome life's challenges and truly thrive. As a new-generation content creator for some of the most respected Christian brands in the world, Benjamin helps people grow deeper in their faith and reach higher in life. He is married to his high school sweetheart, Cindi, and they have three sons. For more about the author, go to benjaminwindle.com.